Saint Worship and
the Worship of Mary

Orestes A. Brownson

Saint Worship
and the
Worship of Mary

Why Devotion to the
Saints Makes Sense

SOPHIA INSTITUTE PRESS®
Manchester, New Hampshire

Saint Worship and the Worship of Mary was originally published in 1963 by St. Anthony Guild Press, Paterson, New Jersey. This 2003 edition by Sophia Institute Press® includes editorial revisions, and Part II has been abridged and divided into individual chapters.

Copyright © 2003 Sophia Institute Press®

Cover design by Theodore Schluenderfritz

Sophia Institute Press®
Box 5284, Manchester, NH 03108
1-800-888-9344
www.sophiainstitute.com

Imprimi potest: John E. Byrne, C.PP.S., Provincial
Nihil obstat: Donald W. Kraus, Ph.D., Censor Librorum
Imprimatur: John J. Wright, Bishop of Pittsburgh
April 19, 1963

Library of Congress Cataloging-in-Publication Data

Brownson, Orestes Augustus, 1803-1876.
    Saint worship and the worship of Mary : why devotion to the saints makes sense / Orestes A. Brownson.
        p. cm.
    ISBN 1-928832-88-1 (pbk. : alk. paper)
    1. Saints — Cult. 2. Mary, Blessed Virgin, Saint — Devotion to. I. Title.
BX2333 .B76 2003
235'.2 — dc21   2003013841

03 04 05 06 07 08 09 10 9 8 7 6 5 4 3 2 1

Contents

Part I: Saint Worship

Part II: The Worship of Mary

☞

Foreword

In 1865, when the Very Reverend Edward Sorin, founder of Notre Dame University, and later Superior General of his congregation, established the *Ave Maria*, he appealed to Orestes Brownson to enrich its pages with some of the gems of thought and composition for which the distinguished Catholic philosopher was known.

In response, Brownson began a series of articles on the veneration that Catholics pay to the saints, particularly to the Mother of God. After Brownson's death, years later, his son Henry collected the articles and incorporated them into Volume VIII of his father's *Works*. But as Brownson's *Works* are now extremely difficult to come by, it has been thought that it would be a genuine service to reprint these articles for the public at large in a popular form. The closely related separate article entitled "The Worship of Mary," written in 1853 and also found in Volume VIII of Brownson's collected *Works*, is included here with the *Ave Maria* series.

In treating this subject, Brownson seldom or never gave way to emotionalism or sentimentality, but wrote rather as the philosopher who wished to show that the honor or veneration that Catholics pay to the saints is warranted, and indeed called for, on the grounds of the strictest theological reasoning. He had in mind that he was writing mainly for Catholics living in a country where Catholic practices were widely regarded as superstitious and were often under attack. In this matter, as in all his other writings as a Catholic apologist, he wrote with the twofold design, of strengthening the faith of his fellow Catholics and of demonstrating its intrinsic rightness to their adversaries. It would be difficult to find anywhere a tract that defends Catholicity more thoroughly and forcefully against the imputation of idolatry or superstition, in the honor it pays the Mother of God and the saints, than the treatises presented here.

In his effort to present his line of thought on this subject with all possible clearness, when first publishing it serially, Brownson sometimes repeated, in one form or another,

ideas he had developed in a previous issue. This tended to
bridge the installments and thus to aid the general conti-
nuity of thought. It has been deemed advisable not to retain these recapitulations in presenting his thought as a
single whole. Their original purpose no longer holds, and
their elimination gives to the general text an easier flow
for the present reader. On the same principle, some pas-
sages have been dropped from the essay "The Worship of
Mary" that are virtually identical with those appearing in
"Saint Worship." Finally, a very few minor alterations
have also been made to accord with the changing genius
of the English language. All has been done only in the interest of presenting Brownson's message in its intrinsic
force and eloquence in the hope that it will reach the
wide readership it so richly deserves.

Thomas R. Ryan, C.PP.S.
Feast of the Annunciation
of the Blessed Virgin Mary
March 25, 1963

Saint Worship and
the Worship of Mary

Part I

Saint Worship

⁀

Chapter One

Supreme, distinctive worship
is given only to God

All love is demonstrative. It seeks always to express itself, and the expression of love is worship. From love springs alike the worship of God and of all that is godlike or related to the supreme and central object of love.

In every age of the Church, saint worship has never come about by virtue of any positive precept, but from the overflowing of the pious Catholic heart. It is, if I may so speak, a necessity of Catholic piety. The love with which the regenerate and faithful soul is filled cannot be satisfied without it. That love must worship, and it must worship the universal God: God in Himself and God in His works, all of which, through His creative act, partake of His divine being and are, through the medium of the act, identified with Him. The worship would seem to the soul incomplete, defective, if it did not embrace the creature with the Creator, and especially if it did not include the saints, who, of all His creatures, are the nearest and dearest to Him. The heart that does not include them in its love of God, and honor them in its honor of Him, may break no positive command, but it may be assured that it has at best only a stingy love and has no reason to applaud itself for either its logic or the fullness of its devotion.

Protestant sects regard the worship we render to the saints, especially to the Blessed Mother of our Redeemer, as idolatry. But this is because they do not consider that to worship God in His creatures, especially His saints, redeemed by His blood and sanctified by His grace, is still to worship God; or that the worship we render to the saints is never that which we offer to God Himself. Supreme worship is due to God alone, and to give it to another is idolatry, is treason to the Most High, to the Majesty of Heaven and earth. None know this better than Catholics.

But *worship* is a general term, which includes not only different degrees, but different species. The word is from the Anglo-Saxon *weorthscipe*, which means simply the state or condition of being worthy of honor, respect, or dignity. And to worship is to ascribe worth, honor, dignity, or excellence to someone literally, to honor someone — it may be God, the magistrate, or simply any man — for his office, station, acquirements, or virtues. The word itself may with like propriety designate the religious homage we owe to God, the reverence we give to the saints, or the civil respect we pay to persons in authority, whether in Church or state. Idolatry is not in rendering worship to men, but in rendering to them the worship that is due to God alone.

Some Protestants overlook this fact and, when they see us Catholics unmistakably worshiping saints — and perhaps rendering the saints as high a worship as that which they in reality render to God Himself — conclude, rashly, that we are idolaters. But they seem not to be aware that the supreme and distinctive act of worship of God is sacrifice, and that we offer sacrifice never to any saint, but to God alone. That Protestants should regard our saint worship as idolatrous is not strange or surprising. Having rejected the Sacrifice of the Mass, they have no sacrifice to offer, and therefore really no supreme, distinctive worship of God; and their highest worship is of the same kind, and not much higher, if at all, than that which we offer to the saints themselves. Doubtless, so-called orthodox Protestants hold that a sacrifice, an all-sufficient sacrifice, has been offered by our Lord in offering Himself on the Cross. But in their view, this sacrifice was completed, finished in the past, and is not an offering continuously made and therefore made now on our altars, as really and as truly as on Calvary. In regard to men now living, according to them, there is no sacrifice to offer and, consequently, no supreme, distinctive worship of God. Hence their churches have a table, but no altar except by a figure of speech, as it is only by a figure of speech that they commune of the body of our Lord.

Their divine service or religious worship consists chiefly of prayer and the singing of hymns or psalms, and comprises in kind nothing that is not perfectly lawful to offer to men. It is lawful to love our neighbor, to honor the magistrate, to pray to those in authority, to sing the praises of the conquering hero, and to confide in our friends. What in all this is distinctively religious worship, or that which can be given only to God?

But because Protestants have, and believe in, no higher worship, it does not follow that there is none higher, or that we do not have it. It is not good logic to argue that because they in their worship anthropomorphize God, we in ours divinize the saints. The Sacrifice of Calvary, perpetuated in the Sacrifice of the Mass, really and truly is the supreme, distinctive worship of God. As we have the true spiritual worship and offer it only to God, we can accept and encourage the overflowings of the pious heart toward the saints without any danger of idolatry.

The Holy Sacrifice is never offered to a saint, not even to the Mother of God. Our churches and altars are all dedicated to God alone. Those that bear the name of some saint are, like all the others, dedicated to God and simply placed under the patronage or intercession of the saint. The saints honored by offices in the church service are not the direct object of the worship. The sacrifice is offered to God in thanksgiving for them: the prayers are all addressed directly to God, and only the saints' intercession is invoked. So, too, in the authorized litanies of the saints and of the Blessed Virgin, the saints are indeed invoked, but nothing is asked of them but their prayers for us, which is no more than we all ask daily of our pastors, of our friends, and of one another. And why may we not ask as much of a saint in Heaven as of a sinful mortal on earth? Is the saint less living or less dear to God?

But saint worship does not simply spring from the exuberance of Catholic piety, is not simply an instinct or a spontaneous outburst of the Catholic heart. It has a reason in the deepest mysteries of our religion, and there is a profound philosophy in it, undreamed of by those who neglect it. It is no excrescence on the Christian religion, no corruption of the simplicity of primitive worship, but a normal development that has its root in the very essence of the Christian system, or the divine plan of creation, redemption, and glorification. It is defensible not only to pious affection, but also to the understanding, and rests on the deepest philosophical and theological principles that we know by either reason or revelation. The Christian religion is catholic; all its principles are catholic; and for everything in it or pertaining to it, there is a catholic reason. *Catholic* means "whole" and "universal," because it embraces the whole. The Christian religion is a systematic whole, and all its parts cohere and are inseparable parts of a complete whole. The catechism is supremely logical, is a dialectic whole, and no part can be denied without denying the whole.

The worship of the saints does not stand alone, but rests on a principle as universal, as integral, and as essential as the worship of God. The command "Love thy neighbor as thyself" rests on the same principle or ground as the command "Love God." There are two senses in which we may consider saint worship: the first, as the worship of God in His saints; the second, as the worship of the saints for what they are personally, or what nature and they themselves, by the grace of God, have made them.

⤳

Chapter Two

God invites us to worship Him in His creatures

No one can be at all familiar with the Scriptures without being struck by the frequency and the loving manner in which our God calls upon us to worship Him in His works, both in the material universe and in His saints. The Psalms of David especially are full of these touching invitations.

There is a profound philosophy, as well as true and evident piety, in such worship. God is in His creatures, as well as they in Him. It is He who creates all things from nothing by the power of His own word, and all creatures exist by Him, and in Him have their being. The pantheist has a truth, a great truth, but unhappily he misinterprets and misapplies it. This truth is that God is immanent as first cause in all His works; the error is in identifying God's works with God Himself — in denying their real, substantial existence.

God does not create existences as man makes a watch, which, when wound up, may be left to go of itself. He remains always efficaciously present in them, and it is His creative act that calls them into existence and continues them in existence, and gives them their life and activity. Hence the apostle tells us, "In him we live, and move, and are," or "have our being,"[1] which is literally true. No creature has its being in itself, for any existence that has its being in itself is self-existent, and therefore is God. The creature exists from God, and therefore has its being in God, or God in its being. Nothing exists without being, and as God is the universal, eternal, immutable, and only being, every creature does and must in its degree participate in God, and be, in a participated sense, divine.

This is the truth that the pantheist misapprehends and misapplies. The creature is not God, any more than the

---

[1] Acts 17:28. The biblical quotations in these pages are taken from the Douay-Rheims edition of the Old and New Testaments. Where applicable, quotations have been cross-referenced with the differing names and enumeration in the Revised Standard Version, using the following symbol: (RSV =).

act is the actor. But in like manner, as the act is only by the actor, and the actor enters into the act, so does God enter into His creature, and it exists only by participating in His being. I shall, when I come to speak of the worship of the saints in reference to their own personal merits or worth, show that creatures have a substantial existence distinguishable, although inseparable, from God and are, as philosophers say, second causes, capable, through the efficacy of the first cause, of acting from their own central life or activity. Here, however, I wish to fix attention on their intimate relation to God and their participation in His essence.

The pantheist is right in asserting the immanence of the creative act and, so far, the identity of the creature with the Creator, but he is wrong in supposing the Creator directly immanent as being, instead of being immanent only through the medium of His creative act, or in the respect that the actor enters into his act, or the act necessarily partakes of the essence of the actor. The pantheist is therefore wrong in supposing that the creature has, in himself, in the secondary and relative sense, no real action or productive force. By virtue of the creative act of God, every creature participates in the divine being or essence; and as God in His essence is triune, all His creatures in some sense reproduce or imitate, each in its order or degree, the holy and ineffable Trinity.

Hence, all religions and all philosophers recognize in some form the sacred triad. It enters into all things, into the human mind, into the human heart, and is the real type and basis in reasoning of what logicians call the syllogism. Many a syllogism has been constructed to demonstrate the impossibility of the Trinity, but if there were no Trinity, the syllogism itself would be false. In like manner, if there were no God, there could be no atheist. The creature partakes of, and in some manner reveals, the divine essence. The creature, the participant, is not God, but that in which the creature participates is God, is literally and truly the divine essence. As God in His very essence is the being, as distinguished from the substantive existence, of every creature, He can be worshiped without idolatry in everything He has made. God is everywhere and in everything, and nothing is without Him, and everywhere and in everything He is God, and to be worshiped as such.

Moreover, we know God and can, until glorified, know and therefore worship Him only through the medium of His works — His works of creation and revelation. We do not and cannot know God in this life as He is in Himself; we can know Him only as He enters into His works and manifests Himself through them — His works of nature and of grace.

The God manifest in creation and in whom all creatures participate is the one living and true God, and infinitely more than creatures manifest. But we know Him only as He manifests Himself, and only so much of Him as He manifests through them. We know they do not exhaust Him, that He is beyond and above them, even beyond and above all that the Gospel reveals of Him. But in the respect that He transcends them, He is to us above the intelligible, and we can worship Him only as He manifests Himself in and through them. Through them — nature and grace — we know He is, and is infinitely more than they reveal; but it is only in them that we, as it were, touch Him, and lay our heads on His bosom, or prostrate ourselves before Him and kiss His feet.

All things partake of Him, and hence, in all things is something sacred and divine, and this teaches us that nothing is to be condemned or despised. Something of God, if I may so speak, enters into every creature, into the animal, the plant, the mineral, or, as men say, brute matter. All is instinct with life and activity, and in all life and activity are present the power and goodness, the very being, of God, the Creator and Preserver. Hence the sympathy of all great saints with the lower creation, and the sort of brotherhood with man that St. Francis of Assisi[2] recognized in animals, beasts, birds, fish, and the humble worm — a brotherhood authorized by the most profound philosophy, as well as by the most ardent and diffusive charity. In a word, God is in the worm, the sparrow, the lamb, the lily, the rose, the ruby, the diamond, as in man and angels, and the true lover of God delights to trace Him in all things, and in all to render Him homage.

Out of this profound truth that God is everywhere and in everything have sprung all the beautiful and graceful mythologies of the ancient gentile world. The error of these mythologies was that they mistook the participant for the participated, or confounded the creature with the Creator. Instead of seeing the one creative divinity in every fountain and grove, they peopled the fountain and grove with nymphs and naiads, dryads and hamadryads, and made every existence a divinity. They worshiped the rivers and the ocean, the winds and the storms, the forests and the mountains, "four-footed beasts and creeping things"[3] and

[2] St. Francis of Assisi (1182-1226), founder of the Franciscan Order.

[3] Rom. 1:23.

gave to the creature the glory due only to the Creator. The Gentiles were inexcusable; they blinded themselves, for the true God was known. "For the invisible things of Him from the creation of the world are clearly seen, being understood by the things that are made — His eternal power also and divinity."[4] Yet in all those mythologies, the worship of nature, of its various objects, and its generative and destructive forces, which gave birth to the most obscene and abominable rites, was at bottom only the perversion of the truth that God is in His works and is to be worshiped in them. The worship of God in His works, especially in His saints, was older than any mythology, as truth is always older than its abuse or perversion.

Piety, the true religious spirit, seeks God everywhere and in everything, and prostrates itself in worship wherever it finds Him. For it, nature, as a whole and in all its parts, is a temple of the Most High, filled with His *Shekinah*, or glory. And in which of His works does He more clearly reveal Himself than in His saints? The saint is a far higher creation than external nature, and a single saint is more than the whole external universe, for in the saint is completed the work of which nature is only the initial part.

[4] Rom. 1:20.

Saint Worship and the Worship of Mary

The saint participates in God as Creator, Redeemer, Sanctifier, and Glorifier. He manifests God in his works both of nature and of grace, in his initial and completed works, and is the highest and most perfect manifestation of His divinity. How, then, without knowing Him in His saints, are we to attain to our highest and fullest knowledge of God? Or how, without worshiping Him in His saints, can we give Him the worship that is His due, or that fills and satisfies the heart of the worshiper?

The saint is sanctified and made a saint by the incarnate God, and the humanity hypostatically united to the Word in the Incarnation is itself, in union with the Word, from whom it is inseparable, an object of worship. And we are to worship the Son incarnated as we worship the Father. The saint participates in the Son in His humanity as this participates in Him in His divinity. Therefore, to give full and complete worship to the Son, and to God, we must worship Him in the saint, and more especially in her in whose chaste womb the sacred humanity was taken, the queen, or most perfect, of all saints.

We do not invoke the intercession of saints because they are nearer to us than God, but for a reason that will hereafter be given. The saints are not nearer to us than God, nor as near. They are not more compassionate, or more readily touched by our infirmities, or more disposed to aid us, than is God Himself. They do not and cannot interpose between us and God, and however ready they may be to succor us, their readiness, like their power, comes from God, and from Him alone. Nothing can be nearer to us than God, for in Him we live and move and have our being. No creature can be more compassionate or ready to succor us than God Himself, who so loved us that, while we were yet sinners, He gave His only-begotten Son to die on the Cross, that we might have eternal life and not perish everlastingly. He loves us with an infinite love, compassionates us with an infinite compassion; no mother can care so tenderly for her suckling child as God cares for us, and not even Mary can so earnestly desire our salvation as He does.

The principle of all saint worship is primarily in the fact that God is really and truly in His works, in all His works, but more especially in His saints. And He is to be worshiped wherever He is, not alone on Mount Moriah or on Mount Garizim.[5] The only point to be observed is that it is God in the work, not the work abstracted from Him,

---

[5] Cf. John 4:20. Mount Moriah is where Abraham worshiped God; Mount Garizim is where the Samaritans did.

that must be the real object of worship, when worship is taken in its highest religious sense. The worship of God in His works in the sense explained is not idolatry, and so long as there is clearly and distinctly preserved the idea of creation, it can never degenerate into idolatry. The heathen became idolaters because they lost the conception of creation and fell into some form of pantheism, confounding the creature with the Creator.

I shall speak further on of the relative worship of the saints, which, although it grows out of the worship of God in His works, is distinguishable from it. I will direct attention now only to the new aspect it gives to all creation when we learn to connect the works intimately with the Creator, and to recognize the great fact that He is really and truly in them, and that in them all we may see Him, love Him, and worship Him. If I am right in my view, the coolest philosophy comes to defend and justify the most ardent and diffusive piety, and to show that a St. Francis of Assisi, in his most extravagant sympathy with all created things, only proved that his mind and soul lived in the medium of the highest and divinest truth.

All Thy works, O God, partake of Thee and, in Thee, are sacred, holy, divine, and truly filled with Thy loveliness and glory.

Chapter Three

⁓

The saints' free cooperation
with God's will merits our honor

The worship of God in His works, and therefore in His saints, is the worship of God Himself and is distinguishable from the *cultus sanctorum,* or worship, not of God in His saints, but of the saints themselves, practiced by Catholics and authorized by the Church — the worship that Protestants object to as giving to the creature the homage that is due to the Creator. The objection would be valid if we offered to the saints the supreme religious worship we offer to God in the saints, or if we worshiped them *as* God. This, however, is not the fact, as has already been asserted and as will more fully appear in its due place. It suffices here to show that the creature, especially the saint, has worth deserving of honor or worship.

Saint Worship and the Worship of Mary

The basis of the worship of saints is the fact that they have real worth. Worth, wherever it is found, deserves to be recognized and honored, and to recognize and to honor worth is to worship. The question as to the propriety of saint worship resolves itself, therefore, into the question as to the personal worth or merit of the saint. Has the saint so far a hand in his sanctity or worth that it may be called *his*? The question so stated tells us at once why those sectarians who deny free will, or assert irresistible grace, making man purely passive, not personally active in the work of his sanctification, must, to be consistent with themselves, reject all saint worship as idolatry or as giving to the creature what is due to God alone.

To resolve the question fully, we must revert again to the creative act of God. The vital importance of the primal fact that God is the Creator of Heaven and earth and all things therein, visible and invisible, is not sufficiently felt even by many who call themselves Christians. And perhaps nothing is better fitted to keep it fresh in the memory, and to impress it deeply on the heart, than this very practice of saint worship, so often objected to as tending to obscure it; for in losing sight of the ability of the creature to act and merit, we lose sight of creation itself, and fall, consciously or unconsciously, into pantheism.

It is not unworthy of remark here that the principal thing that distinguished the people of Israel from the surrounding nations was precisely the assertion of God as the Creator of everything that exists as in any sense distinguishable from Himself. The Gentiles never wholly lost sight of the unity of God, and underlying and hovering over all ancient mythologies is the great truth of the divine unity. But all nations except the Israelites had lost the tradition of creation. Even in Plato and Aristotle, the noblest representatives of gentile wisdom, you find no trace of it. The great gentile apostasy was not primarily in denying the unity of God, as so many suppose, but in denying His creative act. Hence, Moses begins the book of Genesis by asserting God as Creator; and He tells His people the literal truth: that there is no nation so great, whose gods are so nigh to them, as their God is to their petitions.[6] The gods the heathen worshiped were not creators, nor held to be such.

The modern apostasy is, at bottom, the same as the gentile apostasy. Its essential denial is the denial of creation, which is the essence of pantheism, as that of atheism is the denial of God, not only as Creator, but as being.

[6] Cf. Deut. 4:7.

Saint Worship and the Worship of Mary

There can be no doubt, to the philosophical mind, that the germs of the pantheistic denial were contained from the first in what are called the doctrines of the Reformation, especially in the doctrine of the reformers regarding grace, free will, and human merit. For my part, I am more struck with Luther's bad philosophy than with his bad theology, and it is some relief to find that so wretched a philosopher held the scholastics as well as the councils of the Church in contempt. Protestantism, in its original and essential character, involved the denial of all second causes, at least in the order of grace; and hence, we find the real thinking men among Protestants either tending to return to the Church or pushing on toward the pantheism to which all heresy in every age or nation inevitably tends.

It is therefore of the greatest importance to the cause of truth, sound theology, and philosophy, that we revive and keep fresh in our minds and hearts the first verse of Genesis, and the first article of the Creed.

I have defended the worship of God in His works by showing that He remains as first cause in them, and that they exist only as they participate, through His creative act, in His being. All worship, all religion, is founded on the relation that subsists, by virtue of the creative act, between God and His creatures. Religion is that which binds man to God, and there is no bond but the creative act, of which the worship of God is the recognition. Deny that bond, and religion would have no real basis, and worship would have no reason in the nature of things, but would be artificial, arbitrary, and false.

But the *immanence* of God in His works as their first cause is not the only fact taught us by the creative act; nor is the fact that God in His works is the one living, eternal, and immutable God the only thing it imports us to consider. We have learned, indeed, thus far, that God is nigh unto every one of us, and that it is in Him that we live, and move, and have our being. But if we consider it well, we learn also that, in Him, we *do* live and move, *do* really and truly exist. God creates us, but He creates us as real, substantial existences, inseparable but distinct from Himself; not indeed independent existences when once created, of sufficiency for ourselves, as Epicureans, deists, and not a few modern savants (who exclude God from the world and disconnect providence from the creative act) absurdly maintain; but still, as real, substantial existences who, as upheld by Him, are capable of acting from our own center as second causes, capable of copying or imitating His creative act and producing effects of our own.

Saint Worship and the Worship of Mary

All created things, from the highest to the lowest, are active and really exist so far as they are active. There is no absolute passivity in nature. Whatever is purely passive is null. God, say the theologians, is most pure act. He is act in His very essence, and nothing exists save insofar as, through the creative act, it participates of His essence. All that exists, even what we call brute matter, is essentially active, instinct with life, and, in the order and degree of its life, resembles or represents the living and eternal God.

All that exists, then, is worthy of honor as resembling or representing God, the object of supreme worship; as bearing in some sense and degree the likeness of God — just as we treat with respect the image or picture of a dear, honored friend. All creatures, in that they in their several manners represent or resemble God, have a certain worth and are entitled to some degree of worship. Even the lower creation is not wholly ignoble or worthless, and if it is made to be subservient to man, he is to use it with thankfulness and not abuse it.

The forms and degrees of life and activity are different in the different orders of creation. Some creatures act blindly, as minerals and plants that grow, the water that flows, the winds that blow, the lightning that rends the oak, and the storms that sweep over the land, rouse up the ocean, and lash its waves to fury. These act to an end which they see not, and will not, and move by what are called physical laws. Others act from instinct (as men say to hide their ignorance), but as we may say, from simple intelligence, to an end, *ad finem*, as at least the higher classes of animals. Others still, including man and all existences above him, act not only from intelligence, but also from reason, for the sake of the end: *propter finem*, not merely *ad finem*.

The characteristic of man, or that which distinguishes him from the mere animal, I take it, is reason, not simply intelligence; for I am unable to deny every degree and form of intelligence to such animals, for instance, as the dog, the horse, or the elephant, to say nothing of the beaver, the rat, the bee, and the ant. The scholastics and theologians generally define man to be a "rational animal": animal plus reason. Reason is the moral faculty and includes both intellect and will; it sees and wills the end and acts freely for it. The characteristic of man is not, I should say, activity, life, sensation, and intelligence, which he has in common with animals, but reason, the moral faculty by virtue of which he is a moral existence, capable of moral action.

Moral existences, or existences endowed with reason, are created in the image and likeness of God in a much higher sense than others are. God is intelligent, intelligence itself, and acts not only intelligently, but rationally, for the sake of an end, and an end supremely good. Both as first cause and as final cause, He acts not only rationally, but freely. He freely wills the end and freely creates for it. He is not forced to create by any external or internal necessity, because He is independent, eternally complete in Himself, and sufficient for Himself. He is not forced to create as an internal necessity of His own nature, as Cousin maintains,[7] nor to fill up, complete, or actualize his being, as Hegel, confounding the procession of the three Persons in the Godhead with creation *ad extra*, contends. He cannot, indeed, annihilate or contradict His own being, and if He acts externally at all, He must act as He is, as the apostle assures us when he asserts that "it is impossible for God to lie."[8] But He is free to act, or not to act, and to act as He will, restrained by no internal necessity and hedged in by no real or imaginary laws of nature.

[7] "If God is a cause, He can create, and if He is an absolute cause, He must create": Victor Cousin, *Introd. à l'Histoire de la Phil.*, Leçon 5.

[8] Heb. 6:18.

The saints' free cooperation with God's will

This freedom of God, which pagan philosophy never understood and which so-called modern science so rashly impugns, is the archetype and ground of all human freedom, and in this freedom all moral existences participate through the creative act. The denial of the divine freedom in creating is the denial of creation itself, and the denial of all moral existence. The assertion of that freedom asserts that God may, if He chooses, create moral existences, or creatures capable of acting freely under a moral law, and therefore of having a moral merit or demerit of their own.

That He has created man as such an existence, we know from the general assent of mankind, from divine revelation, and from our own consciousness — especially our own consciences accusing or else excusing us, and which we can no more doubt than we can our own existence. Man, then, has a moral nature and is personally responsible for his actions.

This moral likeness to God, in which man is created, and which renders him, not only active, as all creatures are; not only intelligently active, as many creatures are; but morally active and capable of imitating the divine model in the moral order, is itself, on the principle already established, deserving of honor and respect. It is deserving, that is, of some sort or degree of worship, for the sole reason that it is a likeness, however faint, of the Creator Himself.

But this is not all, nor the special ground of saint worship. God is actively present in all His works, as creating them, enabling them in the order of second causes to act, and sustaining them as the subject of their own acts; but He is not present as their direct subject, as Calvin assumes when he makes God the author of sin. God works in us, giving us the power to will and to do, but the actual willing and doing are our own, both in the order of nature and of grace. Our Lord says, indeed, "Without me you can do nothing";[9] and St. Paul says, "I have labored . . . yet not I, but the grace of God with me."[10] Yet, although we can do nothing without Christ, it does not follow that what we do by Him and for Him is not our doing. And although it is grace that does it, grace dwelling in us, elevating us above our natural selves, and giving us more than our natural power to do, it therefore does not follow that grace does it without the participation of our own activity or the concurrence of our will. Grace, in relation to the supernatural end of man, sustains the subject as an actor in

[9] John 15:5.
[10] 1 Cor. 15:10.

the order of second causes, enables a man to do what, without it, would infinitely exceed his powers; but the doing is his own, as is the merit and the reward, or the demerit and the penalty.

The contrary doctrine, taught by the reformers, involves precisely the same error in the Christian order, or the regeneration, as the denial of creation does in the natural, or initial, order. It denies that the soul is an actor in the work of its own sanctification — denies, that is, in sanctification the existence of second causes. It is simply pantheism, and it denies the creative act by denying that anything is created. In the natural order, we are nothing but what God makes us. Yet we are something, because He makes us something — an actor in the order of second causes, because He makes us such. In the order of grace — the regeneration, or the "new creation," as St. Paul calls it — we are nothing but what grace, or Christ, our Redeemer and Savior, makes us. Yet we are, as in the natural order, something — an actor — because He makes us so. The new creation is not merited, nor was the first. Each is the free act, the gratuitous gift, of God; and in neither is our freedom as secondary cause impaired, but really sustained and confirmed by the very fact that, on the part of God, the act is free and the gift gratuitous. We are what we are by the grace of God, but we *are*, nonetheless, for that. We are able to merit only by virtue of His gratuitous gifts, but that does not deprive us of the ability to merit, because those gifts are precisely what give us that ability.

Now, it is on the ability to act and to merit that the propriety of the worship of the saints rests. That worship implies that God has created men as substantial existences, has created creatures as second causes, and men as moral actors; and therefore it prevents us from losing sight of the fact of creation and falling into pantheism, from confounding the creature with the Creator. It is one of our best practical safeguards against the ancient gentile as well as the modern Protestant apostasy, for the reason and ground of the worship force the worshiper to keep in mind the distinction between the saint as creature and God as Creator. And whenever we find anyone offended at the worship of the saints, especially of Mary, the queen of all saints, we have reason to fear that his conception of God as Creator is growing obscure, and that there is danger that he may go on falling away and make shipwreck alike of his faith and of his soul.

⁀

Chapter Four

The principle of
saint worship is universal

I have shown that it is meet and proper, not only to worship God in His saints, but also to worship the saints themselves for such personal merits or worth as they have acquired by their voluntary concurrence with the divine action in nature and grace. Before I consider what is the actual worship we render to the saints, I must prove that the *principle* of saint worship is held even by people who do not accept the Church.

The principle of saint worship is that saints have merit, and merit is to be honored wherever it exists — a broad and, in some sense, democratic principle, in that it overlooks all the factitious distinctions of birth, race, rank, wealth, or position, to fix the regard on real moral worth. The Church has canonized kings, nobles, military officers of high rank, private soldiers, humble shepherds, poor peasants, and day laborers. Mary is not worshiped as a saint because she was of the royal line of David, but for her personal worth — her real worth, acquired by her uniform concurrence with divine grace. And if she is more honored than any other saint, it is because her merits are greater, as well as her connection closer with the salvation of man.

I have defended or justified the worship of the saints by showing that God has created them second causes, capable of concurring by their own free will with His divine action and, therefore, by the assistance of His grace, of acquiring merit. The saints are they who have well merited, and it would be unjust not to acknowledge it, not to render to them the honor that is their due.

The principle of saint worship is admitted, and the worship, to some extent, is practically rendered, even by those who hold that the saint worship practiced by Catholics is idolatry and superstition. All ages and nations practice in some form and in some degree what Thomas Carlyle calls hero worship, in which, in his quaint way, he tells us there is a moral fitness and a profound philosophy. No small part of the religion of the ancient pagans consisted of

The principle of saint worship is universal

hero worship. No doubt the pagans often honored in their heroes and great men what were really not virtues, and with honors that should never be paid to a creature. But so far as they honored human virtue, or intended to honor it, they recognized the fundamental principle on which our saint worship rests, and differed from us only in its development and application.

Our modern pagans are not insensible to the principles of saint worship and in their own way develop and apply it in practice. And far gone is the nation that fails to recognize and honor worth in its servants! How many American parents have given their children the names, how many counties, towns, cities, villages, and city streets in our country bear the names of its great men — just as in Catholic countries they have the names of the saints.

All of this shows that the principle of saint worship is active in the hearts of non-Catholic Americans, and it is, I need not say, a principle that does honor to human nature. All duty is duty to God; and the basis, the fundamental principle, of the civil order is precisely that of the religious order. All true civil or political principles have their ground and origin in theological principles, and, through the medium of the creative act, they are joined to God.

Saint Worship and the Worship of Mary

We live, and move, and have our being in God, and God, by His creative act, is in us, in all our thoughts, words, and deeds, for without Him we are nothing and can do nothing. The fundamental principle of all human activity in all orders is one and the same. Hence, theologians tell us, grace supposes nature, and it is an error to hold that grace supersedes nature. Grace takes away no natural faculty and adds none; it simply elevates to a new plane our natural faculties and gives them a new power and direction, as we are taught by the Church in her doctrine that our free will concurs in the work of our conversion. In conversion, in justification, in spiritual progress, human nature acts and must act, and on this fact we have grounded the possibility of human merit. Nature is not sufficient of itself, is not complete in itself, for it has in itself neither its first beginning nor its last end, and therefore all natural good is imperfect good. But all Catholic theologians teach that, insofar as it is real, it is good, and hence the proposition that "all the works of infidels are sins" is condemned.

Now, as man exists and acts only by virtue of the creative act of God, all his actions in some sense pertain to the religious order, as being done by virtue of the principle which is the principle of religion itself. Whatever action is right in the natural order, or in the civil order, is included in religion and, to some extent, partakes of its character. The civil virtues are not of themselves sufficient to merit the eternal rewards of Heaven, nor are the civil honors we pay to them, or to statesmen, military heroes, patriots, philosophers, scholars, poets, artists, et cetera, as high as those merited by the great saint who, to the natural, joins the supernatural. But they are religious in the sense that they proceed from the relations of man to God through the divine creative act.

The error of gentilism in its hero worship was not as to the principle underlying it, which was the same as the principle of Catholic saint worship, a principle natural to the human heart and authorized, as we have seen, by its relation to the principle of the worship of God Himself. The error was in the virtues honored and in the honors paid. There is a vast difference between canonization and apotheosis. Canonization simply attests the virtues of the saint and authorizes the faithful to worship, or honor, him *as a saint*. Apotheosis placed the hero among the gods and authorized his worship *as a god*. To the saint we pay only such honors as are due to a man who, concurring with divine grace, is sanctified and glorified — that is, completed, made perfect in Christ our Lord. To the divinized hero, the heathen paid divine honors, which are not and cannot be due a simple creature, however great or holy.

Then again, the virtues honored by the heathen in their hero worship were often no virtues at all, or, if virtues, were not virtues of the highest order. Take, for example, Hercules, Theseus, Romulus, Indra, Woden, or Thor, and the legend presents you no example worthy of imitation; no virtue but simple strength or force, which is, although a good thing, no moral virtue at all, nor anything for which its possessor deserves to be honored, since it is not a merit acquired by the action of his free will, with or without the assistance of grace. I say nothing of the vices, the crimes, and the gross demerits ascribed by the legend to the famed heroes worshiped by the Gentiles, because the legend is to a great extent mythical, and these things may perhaps be explained in a pantheistic sense, as symbolizing the productive and destructive forces of nature. I speak here of hero worship proper, or of men deified, not of the worship paid to the gods, beings superhuman by nature, who, as the Scriptures inform us, were all demons, or, as we may say, fallen angels, evil spirits, too often in the history of the world adored as divine, as they are in modern spiritism.

The term *Messiah*, applied in the public honors paid to President Lincoln, so barbarously assassinated, and

The principle of saint worship is universal

likewise to Cyrus W. Field, who, it was supposed, had succeeded in laying a working telegraph across the Atlantic,[11] prove how prone men are, not only to practice hero worship, but, when left to themselves, to fall into the pagan error of confounding men with God and God with men, and to convert even civil honors into idolatry and superstition. The heart, when touched by some deep feeling, or acting under strong excitement, is prone to exaggerate, to run into every species of extravagance. And the Church, by taking charge herself of saint worship, forbidding all private or local canonization, and allowing public honors to be paid only to such as she proposes to the veneration of the faithful — and these to be worshiped with only such offices as she herself prescribes — offers the sole safeguard we can have against this natural extravagance, or against converting the worship into idolatry or superstition.

[11] Brownson was writing soon after Lincoln's assassination and the transmission of the first submarine telegraph message between America and Europe. — ED.

Chapter Five

The saints are perfectly united with God

I have wished to show that the order of nature and the order of grace are based on the same fundamental principles and are in reality two distinct parts of one complete plan in the divine decree, rather than two separate and unrelated orders. The order of regeneration is the complement or completion of the order of generation, and I follow, for myself, the theological opinion that God would have become incarnate even if man had not sinned; although assuredly, in such case, He could not have come to suffer and die for man's redemption. But be this as it may, it is certain that the order of regeneration is teleological and does complete the order of generation. And since man has actually sinned, grace can complete nature only by redeeming it, and redemption and regeneration are, in relation to the individual, simultaneous, whether really distinguishable or not.

Now, we know by supernatural revelation that God is three distinct Persons in one essence. The three Persons are related to each other in the divine being, operating *ad intra* as principle, medium, and end; the Father is principle, the Son is medium, and the Holy Spirit is end and therefore proceeds from both — from the Father as principle and the Son as medium — and thus, so to speak, completes the divine *pleroma,* or consummates *ad intra* the divine being.

God operating *ad extra* after His own idea, which is His essence, is one and indivisible, and therefore in all operations *ad extra* the three Persons necessarily concur, but in diverse respects: the Father as principle, the Son as medium, the Holy Spirit as end, or consummation. The Son, or Word, is the medium of creation. "All things were made by Him, and without Him was made nothing that was made."[12] As essentially God, He is the Creator; as distinctly Son, He is the medium of creation. Hence, the apostle says, by, or *through,* Him all things were made.

We know from revelation that in the fullness of time, the Son — as the medium of all the divine operations to

[12]John 1:3.

complete the creative act and raise man to union with God in Heaven, or to redeem fallen man and, in doing it, to secure him a supernatural beatitude — assumed flesh in the womb of the Virgin Mary, took upon Him human nature, and raised it to be truly and indissolubly the nature of God. As God incarnate becomes the Founder of the teleological order, or, as St. Paul calls it, "the new creation" (but a creation having relation to the end or fulfillment of what is initial and inchoate in Adam in the first order, i.e., the order of generation), there must subsist in this new order between the incarnate Creator and the new creation the same relation that I labored to show subsists between Him and the creature in the first, or initial, creation.

From this we obtain a new ground for saint worship and may learn that saint worship is the best safeguard against that form of naturalism which denies the Incarnation, and with it the whole order of grace and man's supernatural destiny. In the Incarnation, God takes upon Himself our nature and makes it His own. Since the Incarnation,[13] human nature is the nature of the Word; not His divine

---

[13] In this phrase, Brownson speaks of the moment when the Incarnation occurred in time, not of its eternal decree in the council of the Trinity.

nature, but His human nature, yet as truly and as indissolubly His nature as the divine nature itself.[14] This is the mystery of the Incarnation — the mystery of God manifest in the flesh, which no created intellect can comprehend, and which, if I may so speak, exhausts the creative power of God that, infinite as it is, can go no further.

By the Incarnation, then, human nature becomes an object of supreme worship. As Christians, we honor the Son as we honor the Father, the Son of man as we honor the Son of God; for the Son of man and the Son of God are henceforth one, and the same God is present in His saints, not only by His creative act, and by the gifts of His grace, but by identity of nature. They have a natural

[14] As Brownson later indicates, the mystery of the Incarnation does not mean that the Word assumed human nature in the abstract. In the hypostatic union, the Divine Person, the Word, assumed a perfect individual human nature, so that Christ Jesus is perfect God and perfect man. It is only by faith and Baptism that Christians are reborn spiritually after the likeness of Christ, made partakers of His divine nature, temples of the Holy Spirit, and adopted children of God the Father. Since, however, it is the will of God that all men be transformed according to the image of His Son, humanity is destined, in germ, to the deification mentioned on the opposite page by Pope St. Leo the Great (d. 461; Pope from 440 and Doctor). — ED.

relation to Him. This nature, human nature itself, in the language of Pope St. Leo the Great, has been deified, and therefore, in the order of regeneration — I almost fear to write it — it is to be worshiped as the nature of God.

Tremendous thought! What meaning does it give to the injunction "Honor all men," and how forcibly does it bring home to us the fact that, "if any man says, I love God, and hateth his brother, he is a liar, and the truth is not in him"![15]

It is, however, human *nature* that is deified, not the individuals of the race. Individually, human nature is hypostatically united to God only in the man Jesus Christ. As individuals, the saints are sons of God only by adoption, and while their nature is deified and worshiped as the nature of God, and therefore with divine honors, they as individuals can be honored only with a relative or secondary worship, not as God, but as related to Him through His human nature. Nevertheless, this relation itself deserves to be recognized and honored in them as well as in Him.

The itinerary of the soul is from God as first cause, through regeneration in Christ, to glorification, or supernatural union with God as final cause. The saints are those

[15] 1 John 4:20.

who, by their concurrence with the gifts and graces of God, have completed their journey, finished their course, and attained to their supreme beatitude, their crown of glory. They are united to God by identity of nature, by spiritual conformity, and the closest union possible, short of personal identity; and to refuse to recognize and honor it would be a gross indignity to the Word made flesh and to the whole principle of the new creation or order of regeneration. The chief ground of our saint worship, after all, is in the relation of the saints in their nature to the nature of God. This relation is initial indeed in all men, since human nature is one and the same in all, but consummated, completed, or perfected only in the saints, who are individually conformed to and united with God and made "partakers of his divine nature,"[16] so that they are really, in a secondary or imitative sense, Christs, and sons of God, as Christ is the Son of God.

It is now easy to understand the *hyperdulia*, or superior worship, we render to Mary. It is not solely because, through the gifts and graces of God, her personal merits are greater, but because her relation to the human nature of God is closer and more intimate and therefore entitled

[16]2 Pet. 1:4.

to a larger share in the honor we give, and are required to give, to that nature as assumed by the Word. It was from her that God took His human nature, and in doing so, He took that nature to be His own; He raised her to the dignity of Mother of God. The closest relation possible, save the hypostatic, is that between mother and son, and therefore Mary, by her natural relation to the human nature of God, deserves a higher honor than any other saint, and the highest below that given to God Himself. We, then, in our *hyperdulia,* on the strictest philosophical and theological principles, give Mary only the honor that is her due, and with our best efforts we cannot so highly honor her as God honors her.

Because the worship of the saints in general and of our Lady in particular is based on the Incarnation, its practice tends to keep living and active in us the great fact of our religion — "The Word was made flesh" — on which our redemption, our salvation, and all our hopes of final beatitude depend; and almost universally, the neglect of saint worship is followed by loss of faith in the Incarnation. The sects that reject saint worship hardly in a single instance remain orthodox on the capital point of our Faith.

Chapter Six

When we honor the saints, we honor God

Man's itinerary is from God by way of creation as first cause, and to God as final cause without absorption in Him. All religions, the false as well as the true, assert this itinerary, or procession of existences from God, and their return to Him. But the ancient and modern heathen religions, especially the Hindu and the Buddhist, teach that the procession of existences from God is by way of emanation or generation, which is the radical assumption of pantheism, and that their return to Him is absorption in Him, the return of the stream to its source. This denies all individual existence and individual or personal immortality.

All the pagans early lost the tradition and even the conception of the creative act, and Christianity — counting the Jewish and Christian religions as substantially one and the same religion — is the only religion the world has ever known that is not pantheistic.[17] It asserts the procession of existences from God to be by virtue of the divine creative act, and their return to Him to be without absorption in Him or loss of individual or personal existence. It is I individually, in my own personal identity, who will live again, either in Heaven or in Hell.

All religion pertains to this second part of the soul's itinerary. It teaches man his origin, but as the condition of his knowing and aspiring to his end in God. Its real mission is to show man his obligation of seeking that end by the exercise of his reason and will, and to supply him with the means necessary for attaining it. All religion is teleological and has reference solely to the end, to the perfection, the consummation, of man's existence as a creature of God and a free, moral, and rational activity. The word *religion* is probably from *religare*, to bind again, for as creation binds us to God as first cause, so religion binds us again or anew to God as final cause.

This return to God as final cause, as our last end, our supreme good, or beatitude (all terms meaning practically

[17]Islam is apparently an exception to Brownson's generalization here.

the same thing) is possible only through the Incarnation. The Incarnation is the only medium of this return and final union with God; equally so, whether we hold that, if man had not sinned, God would or would not have become incarnate. The only Mediator between God and men is the man Christ Jesus, and there is no name but His, under Heaven, given among men whereby we can be saved.[18] He who denies the Holy Trinity denies the Incarnation, and he who denies the Incarnation denies the possibility of man's returning to God, fulfilling his destiny, or attaining to beatitude. Saint worship has, as we have seen, its chief ground in the relation that the saints bear to the Word made flesh, or God incarnate. It pertains, chiefly at least, to the teleological order, the return of existences to God and beatitude in union with Him.

I have shown that the worship of saints is founded on the great mysteries of our religion and is the best possible safeguard of faith in those mysteries themselves, especially the great facts of creation and Incarnation, which the heathen lose sight of, pervert, or travesty. Indeed, all Catholic practices, growing as they do out of the great principles of Faith, have a direct tendency to keep faith fresh, living,

[18]Cf. Acts 4:12.

and life-giving in the heart and soul. There is a profound logic, a living reality, in all that the Church commands or approves. The Real Presence, if I may so speak, is everywhere, at once a particular and a universal truth. Hence, our religion is always coherent, self-consistent, and, when embraced and observed, efficient. It is always real, founded on the truth and reality of things. Hence, it appears to those who study it without believing it a masterpiece of human wisdom. A masterpiece of wisdom it is, but of the wisdom of God, not of man, for man was never equal to its invention or discovery.

But not only for the reasons assigned is saint worship religious and serviceable to religion. It is religious because the honor we pay to the saints redounds to the honor of God. We worship God in them, and we worship them in God and for God. We do not honor the saints because they are nearer to us than God or because they more readily sympathize with us. As was said earlier, this is not true. God is infinitely nearer our souls, and infinitely more tender and loving, than any saint. The saints' power, tenderness, and love come from God, return to God, and are His. Mary is indebted to God for all those qualities and virtues we love and honor in her. Her personal merit is solely in her voluntary concurrence, by the aid of divine grace, with divine grace. If we honor the saints in a certain sense for their own merits, we know that those merits are only the fruits of God's gifts, and in rewarding them, He only crowns His own gifts. Our great reason for honoring them is that God Himself honors them. How can we be godlike if we honor not whom God honors? How can we really love God if we love not whom He loves?

The worship of the saints, then, is connected with the worship of God and bears the same relation to it that the saint himself bears to Him who has created, redeemed, regenerated, and glorified him. As we cannot love God fully without embracing in our love all that He loves, so we cannot give Him the honor that is His due without honoring all whom He honors.

Chapter Seven

Praying to God
justifies praying to saints

From the fact that we pray to God to grant us favors through the intercession of the blessed Mary ever-virgin, and of other saints honored by the Church, I infer, first, that the honors paid to the saints are religious, not merely civil; secondly, that we do not pray to the saints on the supposition that we cannot pray directly to God Himself, or that the saints are nearer to us, in closer relation to us, and more ready to hear and assist us; and, thirdly, that what, in the worship of the saints, we ask of them is their intercession, or simply their prayers. We do not ask the saints, not even the blessed Mary, for pardon, for mercy, for grace, or blessings of any sort, as things in their power to grant. We simply ask them to aid us by their prayers, or to intercede with God to obtain these things for us from Him from whom comes every good and perfect gift.

What we ask of the saints in glory is only what we may and do ask of one another while living in the flesh. Many years ago, before I had the happiness of being received into the communion of the Catholic Church, I was, as most Protestants who retain some respect for religion are, in the habit of frequently closing my letters to my friends with the words "Pray for me." One day, writing to a very dear friend, but one who was not precisely a saint, I concluded in this same way. I did so from the force of habit, but I had no sooner written the words than a thought suddenly struck me, and I exclaimed to myself, "There is the justification of the Catholic practice of invocation of saints. Here I am asking a sinful mortal to pray for me. How much, rather, should I ask the prayers of a beatified saint in Heaven, always in the presence of God!" From that moment to this, I have had no difficulty with the invocation of saints, nor hesitated to ask them to pray for me. And long before my conversion, I had specially invoked the prayers of our Lady, and I have no reason to doubt that her intercession obtained for me what I needed: the grace of faith and docility, whether I have profited by it or not. For from that day, my mind began to open to the truth of our holy religion, and it seemed as if the dark clouds that had hidden its beauty from my view began to part and roll back and disclose the splendor beyond, and nothing was easier than to believe.

But still it is asked what need is there to pray the saints at all, and why not pray directly to God Himself, since He is infinitely nearer to us, and more ready and able to help us, than any saint is or can be?

I answer that Catholics do pray directly to God, and perhaps even more than those who reject prayers to the saints do. And I might ask, in our turn, why pray even directly to God, since He knows all our wants better than we ourselves know them, knows what we are going to pray for before the prayer is formed in our own heart, and is infinitely more willing to help us than we are to ask His help?

The same principle that justifies prayer to God justifies prayers to the saints to intercede for us, and certainly nothing in religion is more certain than that prayer is enjoined as a duty, and that if offered not amiss, it avails much. There is not, and never was, a religion without prayer, and prayer is an integral part of every religious service, in every age and nation. On what principle does it depend? Is there a universal, or catholic, reason for it?

Saint Worship and the Worship of Mary

Every dogma and every practice enjoined or approved by the Church rests on a catholic, or universal, principle, and therefore she *is* really, not merely *called*, the *Catholic* Church. She is the Catholic Church because all her doctrines are catholic or universal principles, always and everywhere true, whether we speak of the order of nature or of the order of grace, and all her authorized practices have their reason in these universal principles. The principles of the order of grace are the principles of the order of nature, for grace does not contradict, extinguish, or supersede nature, but presupposes it, accepts it, and completes, consummates, or fulfills it. "I am not come," said our Lord, "to destroy, but to fulfill."[19] Nature has its fulfillment in grace, generation in regeneration and glorification. God, if I may so speak, creates always after one and the same divine plan and is, both in His ordinary and His gracious — extraordinary — providence, fulfilling one and the same original design. He is the infinite and eternal logic, and although infinitely free in all His external acts, alike from outward coercion and inward necessity, He is never illogical, inconsequent, arbitrary, or capricious in any of His works. He never deviates from the plan His

[19]Matt. 5:17.

own wisdom has devised, never alters or amends it, but carries it out with infinite self-consistency, both as a whole and in all its parts.

Hence the uniformity, regularity, and harmony of the universe, and the universality and immutability of what are called the laws of nature; hence, too, the difficulty that men who devote themselves to the study of the natural sciences find in admitting miracles, or the supernatural facts of our religion, which seem to them to be deviations from the uniformity of the plan of creation, inconsequences in the divine action, so contrary to reason that no possible evidence can prove them, for no evidence can rise higher than reason itself. Their difficulty arises from not knowing or not reflecting upon the truth that the miracles and supernatural facts are in the *order* of the supernatural, and that this supernatural order does but carry on in the same line and complete the natural; or in other and more precise terms, that grace simply fulfills nature (or completes what is not ultimate, but inchoate or initial, in the world they study), and is not more or otherwise supernatural than the creative act itself. Nature is supernatural in its origin and end, and the natural is only that which God does mediately, through the ministry or agency of second, or created, causes. There is in what we here assert the principle of the harmony of faith and reason, of the truths of revelation and the truths of science. The principles of both are the same, and they differ only in the fact that faith reveals their origin and ground in the divine mind and is the medium of their development and application beyond the power of human reason.

Whenever we find any proposition or fact that we can refer to no catholic, or universal, principle, we may always rest assured either that it is false or that we do not understand it, have failed to seize its real meaning; for every real fact, every true proposition, has a universal as well as a particular sense. It is on this ground that the great Fathers and Doctors of the Church seek always in the Holy Scriptures more than the simple historical sense and regard the moral and spiritual sense that transcends it as by far the more important. We see this especially in Origen and St. Augustine (although in the works of Origen as transmitted to us there are some grave errors).[20] We see it in all the Christian mystics, from whom, if we know how to read them, we may best seize the spirit and inner sense of religion, for they give us our Faith in its synthesis, as a living

[20]Origen (184-254), theologian and biblical scholar; St. Augustine (354-430), Bishop of Hippo.

whole, not simply in detached propositions and isolated particulars.

All the works of God are at once particular and general, and every particular fact is at once a fact and a sign or symbol; and it is chiefly as a sign, as significant of a universal principle, that it deserves to be studied, meditated on. He who sees in the Holy Scriptures only the literal meaning determined by grammar and lexicon has never learned to read the written word of God, and the philosopher who has never looked "through nature up to nature's God"[21] knows as little of nature as he knows of the *Divine Comedy*, who has simply learned its letters and syllables, without being able to join them together in words.

Nature is real, not merely ideal or phenomenal; but while real, it expresses or symbolizes a higher reality than its own. It is the characteristic of genius to see, through the sign, that higher reality, and to see and express it under the form of the beautiful is the province of the true artist, the true poet. There is always more in every fact and under all appearances than those minds dream of which stop with the literal, material fact, the mimetic (to borrow a term from Plato), and it is the good side of

[21] Alexander Pope, *Essay on Man*, Epistle 4, line 331.

modern transcendentalism that it is aware of this great truth. But unhappily it forgets that the material, the mimetic, although symbolizing the spiritual, is itself real, not, as they hold, a mere appearance.

Chapter Eight

∽

The intercession of saints
is part of God's plan

It is impossible not to pity our poor materialists who see no existence, no reality, that transcends the sensible order. How little they know or dream of the riches and beauty, the life and grandeur, of God's universe! For them "a primrose by a river's brim"[22] is a primrose and nothing more: it symbolizes to them no reality beyond itself.

The unbelieving Jew saw in Mary only a lowly Hebrew maiden, or the wife of Joseph the carpenter; and yet, while all that, she was the Mother of God, the queen of angels, and the most glorious of the creatures of God. The same carnal-minded Jew saw nothing in our Lord Himself as He

[22]William Wordsworth, "Peter Bell," Part I, stanza 12.

traveled over Judea and Galilee, poor and destitute, with not whereon to lay His head, but the carpenter's son;[23] and yet He was the Lord of glory, the Majesty of Heaven and earth, and the Creator and Governor of the world. To the literalist, who sees nothing beyond the letter, the sacred emblems, the consecrated elements, are simply bread and wine; and yet they are, under the material forms of bread and wine, the Body and Blood, the soul and divinity, of the incarnate God, who gave Himself for us. Catholicism teaches and finds, so to speak, the Real Presence every-where, in everything; all facts, all events, each in its own order and degree, are symbols of truths that infinitely transcend them, and the elect soul regenerated by the Holy Spirit is really joined by faith to that world of incon-ceivable joy and bliss which awaits the just and is the be-atitude of the saints. For faith, says the apostle, "is the substance of things to be hoped for, the evidence of things that appear not."[24]

In the great truth I here insist upon is the key to the marvelous wisdom, even in things of the world, so often met with in saints who live wholly retired and in solitude.

[23]Matt. 8:20; 13:55.
[24]Heb. 11:1.

These men do not spend their lives in forming acquaintance with mere outward facts or with the productions of other men's brains. They meditate on the facts before them, penetrate their meaning, and grasp the universal truth they symbolize. A soul that has learned to meditate finds all nature opened, unveiled to its view, and matter enough in a single spear of grass to charm, delight, instruct, edify, and elevate it for years; for to the heart opened by faith, nature is full of God, and God is the fountain of all science, wisdom, life, and joy. It is not that the holy man is supernaturally or miraculously instructed in a special manner, but that he looks beneath and beyond the literal fact, penetrates the symbol, and finds himself in living relation with a higher and broader order of truth.

Mere external facts give us knowledge and wisdom only as we meditate on them and penetrate their meaning. Animals have senses as keen as men's, and often keener, and they have before them as broad a range of sensible facts; but they lack the mind that sees in the sensible fact the sign of an intellectual and spiritual truth, and that can attain by meditation to the truth signified. The great reason we moderns fall so far below the men of antiquity or of the early ages of the Church is that we speculate more and meditate less, and exercise our understanding less when we meditate. We are active, not contemplative.

But I am suffering the attractiveness of this theme to lead me away from the question before me. I have simply wished to call the attention of my readers to the fact that Catholicism is catholic, that all the doctrines and practices of the Church rest on real and universal principles, and that in neither is there anything narrow, arbitrary, capricious, sectarian, or unreal. Indeed, her dogmas embody the principles, and her practices, her worship in all its parts, are designed to keep alive faith in her dogmas and to realize them in the daily practical life of the faithful.

The principle that the intercession of the saints rests on is that God uses, in completing or perfecting His works, the ministry or agency of second, or created, causes — that is, the agency or ministry of creatures. This is seen in the order of nature no less than in the order of grace. We see it in all the facts of generation, the continuance and multiplication of plants and animals, and in the continuance, multiplication, and growth of the human race itself. So universal is this principle, which goes in the unbelieving world under the name of development, and so uniform and necessary is the part of second causes, that not a few of our scientific men see no need of a first cause and recognize no action but the action of creatures. There is a strong disposition in modern science to explain the origin and progress of all creatures and of the globe itself by their pretended self-sufficient laws of development.

God creates alone, by the word of His power, but, without releasing the creature from dependence on Him, He makes its existence, growth, and well-being dependent, under Him, on others. The child is not born without society, nor reared without his parents' aid. He must have food, and that must be supplied from first to last by others, at first without, and afterward with, his cooperation. Light, air, heat, and moisture are all needed and are administered by nature, also a creature of God. Indeed, the whole created system is a system of mediation and intercommunion.

God gives the harvest, and yet the farmer must till the soil and sow the seed, or he will reap no harvest. Throughout all orders, there are means adapted to the end, and if the means are not used, the end is not gained. So with regard to prayer. It is a means to an end; and it is as unreasonable to suppose the end without the means in this case as in that of the husbandman: God knows from the beginning that the harvest is needed, yet he does not give it unless the appointed means are used. In answering prayer,

He does not change, nor ordinarily work a miracle; we obtain the blessing because we comply with the conditions on which He bestows it and are in a state in which we can receive and profit by it.

The intercession of the saints is in accordance with the same principle, a principle of universal application: that of the agency of the creature in perfecting and completing creation, or the return of existences to God as their final cause.

This is seen in the Incarnation, through which, and through which alone, man is redeemed, elevated, and glorified. In the Incarnation, God makes Himself creature, that the creature may fulfill its destiny, and it is in His humanity that He redeems, regenerates, and sanctifies man, thus making the creature the medium of the whole teleological order. We see the same principle in the institution of the priesthood, and it lies at the bottom of all public divine service. It is clear, then, that the prayers and intercessions of the saints are included in principle in the original plan of the Creator and harmonize perfectly with both the ordinary and the extraordinary providence of God.

Chapter Nine

≈

The saints are concerned for us and can hear our prayers

I have shown that the principle on which the intercession of the saints may avail us is that God, in developing and perfecting, or consummating, His works, uses the agency of second, or created, causes, as in man's redemption and salvation; that is, enables and allows His creatures, in their several orders and according to their nature, to co-operate with Him.

This cooperation in purely physical natures is involuntary and blind — from internal necessity. In rational and moral natures, it is a free cooperation, voluntary — from reason and free will. Hence, God, in the natural world, uses physical agencies and effects His designs by what are called natural laws and, in moral natures, effects them by the ministry of angels and of men. He sends His angel to announce to Mary that she shall conceive by the Holy Spirit, bear a Son, and call His name Jesus, for He shall save His people from their sins.[25] He sends His angel, too, to deliver Peter from prison[26] and communicates revelations to St. John in the Isle of Patmos by a like ministry.[27] He uses men as priests to offer the Holy Sacrifice and to intercede with Him for His people.

This is not because He cannot effect everything by His own direct and immediate action, but because He is good and delights to communicate Himself as far as He is communicable to His creatures, to make them as nearly like Himself as creatures can be like their Creator, and to honor them by making them coworkers with Him and giving them thus a real title to share in His glory. Those who faithfully cooperate with Him in winning souls to Christ, and extending His kingdom on earth, enter, when this work is done, into the joy of their Lord and share His glory. No higher honor can be conferred on a creature than to be permitted to cooperate with God; than to be

[25] Luke 1:26-35.
[26] Acts 12:6-7.
[27] Apoc. 1:1 (RSV = Rev. 1:1).

employed by the King of kings and Lord of lords in His service — to be sent on His errands and to hear from Him the words "Well done, good and faithful servant."[28]

As God delights to honor His creatures by employing them in His service, so He must delight to hear and respond to their intercession for their brethren; for this intercession, although free and willing on their part, and proceeding from their great love of Him and of their fellow creatures in Him, is a part of the service in which He employs them. It honors Him as the source of all good, as the giver of every grace, of every good and perfect gift; honors His love, His tenderness, His mercy, and His compassion for His creatures, to which all intercession is a direct appeal.

These remarks, it seems to me, remove every difficulty that can be supposed to exist, to prayer in general, and the intercession of the saints in particular. Nothing prevents God, if He chooses, from hearing and answering prayers, whether they are our own prayers for ourselves or the prayers of the saints in Heaven for us. Both are in strict accordance with the order of His providence and the principles on which His works are consummated, and on which

[28]Matt. 25:21, 23.

souls are redeemed, sustained, and perfected. In either case, while prayer and intercession are acceptable to God as a loyal recognition of His sovereignty, His freedom, His love, His mercy, and His tenderness and compassion, they are the greatest privilege, and the highest honor to Him who prays or intercedes. Man is privileged; he has at all times access to the presence of his Sovereign, and the ear of his God, and by prayer is elevated, in some sort, to companionship with his Maker. Nothing brings God so near to us, raises us so near to Him, as prayer. And what greater honor could even He confer on His saints than to allow them to take part in His providence by interceding for us and to listen to their prayers and intercessions for those who invoke them? It associates them with Himself in His works of grace.

But the saints have entered into the joy of their Lord, are completely blessed; their happiness is full. Why should they concern themselves with the happiness of others? They are in the presence of God, see Him as He is in Himself, are filled with Him. How can they have any thought for anyone else, or any regard for those they have left behind, or who are still undergoing their probation?

The objection implies too much and also entirely mistakes the nature of the love of God. God is self-sufficing and eternally blessed, happy in Himself. His blessedness can be neither augmented nor diminished. He can be no more, nor happier, with than without creation.

Why, then, does He create? Because He is love, or charity, and love delights to communicate itself; because He would have others love, others share, so to speak, His own blessedness.

The saints are not love, as God is love, but they are as much like Him as creatures can be like their Creator, for they are made partakers of His divine nature and are saints only because they participate in His charity. They must therefore delight to diffuse their love, and desire others to share their blessedness. The beatitude of the saints is not an egotistical or selfish beatitude, which would be no beatitude at all, but a beatitude that has its origin and ground in pure, disinterested love: perfect charity.

The saints are indeed in the presence of their Lord and are filled, satisfied, with His love. But the love of God includes the love of creatures, and no more in Heaven than on earth can one love God without loving his brother also. The saint loves all in God, in whom all live, and move, and have their being. The more one loves God, the more does he love his brother. The beloved apostle says:

"We know that we have passed from death to life *because* we love the brethren."[29] Moreover, our Lord Himself tells us, "'There shall be joy in Heaven upon one sinner that doth penance."[30] The saints in Heaven are not, then, indifferent to us, their brethren on earth. It is the damned, whether angels or men, who cannot love, and therefore is their damnation complete and everlasting.

Hence, I conclude that the saints in glory take a deeper interest in our welfare than we, even the best of us, do in the welfare of one another, because they love more, are happier, and are freed from all care or anxiety for themselves. Their beatitude is consummated and secure. Nothing can destroy or diminish it, and nothing can divert their thoughts to any selfish end. Nothing can divert them from interceding for their brethren — not indeed to augment their own blessedness, or for their own sake, but for the honor of their Creator, the glory of their Redeemer.

But it is alleged, even by persons who call themselves Christians, that however well disposed the saints might be to intercede for us, they cannot hear our invocations, and therefore our prayers to them are vain and even

[29] 1 John 3:14.
[30] Luke 15:7.

superstitious. If they cannot hear us, our prayers to them *are* unquestionably superstitious and not to be tolerated. But why can they not hear us? Are they not living men and women — even more living than when they taber-nacled with us?

Those of the non-Catholic world tend everywhere to heathen, rather than Christian, views of death. They are rapidly losing all real faith in the life and immortality brought to light through the gospel, and darkness and de-spair gather for them once more over the tomb. Nothing is so well fitted to keep living and fresh the Christian faith in the future life as the practice of constantly praying to the saints. There is throughout a close union between Catholic practice and Catholic Faith, and while the Faith gives rise to the practice, the practice keeps alive and real the Faith.

We may remark, too, that they who neglect or reject the practice of praying to the saints soon come to look upon the saints as being as dim and as unsubstantial as the shades asserted by heathen darkness and superstition, and even to doubt all real future personal or individual exis-tence. To Catholic Faith, the saints really live, with a real, personal existence, with all the faculties they had in this life even clarified and strengthened. Why should they be less able to hear us than we are to hear one another? Is it said they are too far from us, so removed from us that our voices cannot reach them? But what do we mean by distance when we speak of saints who have entered into their rest? Are spirits made perfect subject to the accidents of time and space? Time and space pertain only to creatures who are yet on the way, who have not yet returned to God, or actualized their potentiality. When their existence is fulfilled, consummated, the angel of the Lord proclaims that for them time is no more; they have entered eternity. Time and space are only relations, and the saints in glory are not subject to them. They are united to God and, in their unison with Him, are near unto every one of us — nearer, if we love, than they were before they were called home. They are present wherever there is a thought of them.

We must remember that the Communion of Saints is an article of the Christian's creed, and even the Calvinist Doctor Watts sings, "Angels, and living saints and dead/ But one communion make."

There can be no communion where there is no medium of communication. We who live have a medium of communication with those who have gone to their reward and therefore form one communion with them. This medium is Christ Himself, who is the head of every man and whose life is the life of all who are begotten anew by the Holy Spirit. The saints know our thoughts and desires because, seeing God as He is in Himself, they see them reflected in Him as images reflected in a glass, visible in His light, clearly seen and known in it.

This is nothing anomalous. Even in this life, we see and know things only as mirrored to us by the divine light. We see all things in God and through God, because all have their being in Him and are rendered intelligible by the light of His being, which is the light of our reason. There is no more mystery in the way the saints hear our invocations than there is in the way we hear one another. Mystery there is, but it is the same mystery in both cases, and it would be absurd to maintain that we do not hear one another because we cannot explain how we do it. There being a medium of communication between us and the saints, and they and we forming only one communion, one body of our Lord, being members of Him and members of one another, nothing can be more reasonable, more natural even, than that we should invoke their prayers and that they should intercede for us. It is in accordance alike with the order of nature and the order of grace.

Chapter Ten

⤸

God acts directly and through created causes

I have shown that the intercession of the saints is no anomaly in the Creator's plan, but is in strict accordance with His providence, which completes or perfects His works through the agency or ministry of second, or created, causes. Creatures can have no part in the production of existences, that is, in their creation from nothing, but God employs them in developing and completing other creatures. Hence, all existences are active, and, strictly speaking, there is no purely passive existence, no pure passivity, in nature.

In saying that God, in completing or perfecting His works, uses the ministry of angels and men, or employs created agencies — that is, natural causes, so called — I do not mean to be understood as saying that even to this end, He never does anything immediately, directly by Himself, without other mediums than His eternal Word; for miracles are well-attested facts in all ages of the world and prove, among other things, that God is His own law, the Master of nature, and not bound by it. The age has much to say of liberty, and no men are more clamorous for liberty than those who suppose that God is invincibly bound by what they call the laws of nature.

But the basis of all liberty is the liberty of God Himself. To suppose Him subject to natural laws, or the laws of nature, is to suppose Him bound by fate or destiny, as the heathen held their gods to be, and to deny all space for freedom in the universe. Whatever is fixed, invariable, or immutable, in nature or the laws of nature, is not nature, but God, not something above Him, outside Him, and independent of Him, but He Himself, in the plenitude of His own necessary, eternal, and immutable being. He is not free not to be, nor free to be other than He is, but He is always and everywhere free to act as He pleases, through ministries or not, as seems to Him good.

Supernatural intervention, or the direct and immediate action of God in the universe, which is what we call a miracle because it is inexplicable by any natural laws or second causes, as the conception of our Lord in the womb of the Virgin Mary, is not illogical or capricious. In relation to the divine mind, it is as orderly as the growth of a plant, or the gravitation of bodies toward the center of the earth. An act, because free, is not for that reason anomalous, and a principal value of miracles is that they vindicate to us the freedom of God and prove to us that the laws of nature, so called, depend on Him, and not He on them, as from their uniformity and constancy we are apt to suppose. They show us God acting freely, directly, without the agency of second causes, and therefore, they show His freedom, self-existence, and self-sufficingness. They are a direct answer to those who say, "There is no God," or who confound God with nature. They are as credible to him who believes in God as are any of the facts of nature, for they have the same cause, and a sufficient cause, and are provable by the same kind of evidence or testimony. They are no more incredible than creation, which from the nature of the case must be the direct act of God.

But the admission of miracles, the direct supernatural action of God, does not in any sense deny or abridge His action through second causes. A miracle is the act of a power above the laws of nature and not explicable by them. It leaves them to their ordinary operation and simply proves that they do not exhaust the activity of the Creator, and that He survives them in all His infinity, and in all His inexhaustible freedom of action. The heathen believed in prodigies, the intervention of their gods, but had no conception of miracles in the Christian sense, because their gods were not believed by them to be God, and the God they dimly recognized in the darkness, or of whom they retained some faint and fading reminiscences, was to them no creative God. He was, for the most part, in their mythologies resolved into fate, necessity, or destiny, which, says the Emperor Marcus Antoninus, "binds both gods and men."

The Christian believes in God the Creator and therefore can rise to the true conception of a miracle and understand that God may work a miracle without violating the so-called natural order. The miracle transcends nature and reveals the hand, the will, or the power that creates and sustains nature. God can act through the things He has made, and He can act without them, without their cooperation, as is evident from His having been able to create them from nothing. He in fact does act in both ways, and hence, we have always present, in human life, both the natural and the supernatural.

God acts directly and through created causes

The fundamental mistake of those who object to the invocation of the saints is in supposing that God, in the work of our sanctification and perfection in glory, works always without any created medium, or any cooperation on our part with Him. This was the great mistake of the reformers. In their theory, the Incarnation, if not expressly denied, has really no place and practically nothing to do with our regeneration, sanctification, and perfection in glory. The most they can consistently affirm is that the Incarnation was necessary to enable the Son to die on the Cross, and that it was necessary that He should die on the Cross to remove the abstract justice interposed to the pardon of the sinner, or to render it consistent with His majesty for God to pardon and forgive those who had transgressed His law. It has, on their theory, so far as I can conceive, no practical effect on the sinner himself, in redeeming and elevating his nature, and infusing into him a new and higher life, and enabling him to fulfill his destiny, which is union with God in the Beatific Vision. It is at best an expedient for getting rid of a difficulty that never existed, for it was always possible for God, if He chose, to pardon the sinner on repentance and reformation of life. That He does not do so without the Incarnation and redemption through the Passion and Cross of His Son, is not because He cannot, but because He chooses in His infinite love to do something far better for the sinner and to make his fall the occasion of a far greater glory.

Hence we find them, in forgetting this, denying all mediate action of God. Faith is regarded as a direct gift. Regeneration, or the new birth, is the direct work of the Holy Spirit; so is the perseverance of the just and their final salvation. In all, God works immediately, directly, sovereignly; and the creature is purely passive, and in no sense cooperative with the Holy Spirit. Hence, they reject the priesthood, the sacraments, and the whole office of the Church. All this grows out of their denial of the mediatorial system of grace, which has its origin and ground in the Holy Trinity; their rejection, virtual if not formal, of the entire ministry of angels and men. They are in principle, did they but know it, pantheists, denying the reality of second causes, and hence we see everywhere the world of the reformers developing into pantheism.

Chapter Eleven

It is fitting to worship the saints

The Catholic system is the system of the universe, and presents the relations of the universe to its Creator, Upholder, and Governor, as they really are; and hence, the Catholic is saved alike from either atheistic or pantheistic fatalism or nihilism. He neither makes man God nor reduces him to a mere appearance, a bubble on the surface of the ocean. He believes in God the Creator, and in the reality of creation: that God gives real existence to His creatures; that they therefore are, in their order and degree, second causes, cooperative with God in gaining the end for which all things are made. He believes that, when created, they become ministries and agencies in the hands of God to that end; that they are honored in being so employed, and according to their nature and merit can and really do share in the glory of God Himself. Hence, he sees in the intercession of the saints only an integral part of the universal plan of the Creator, as I have heretofore shown, a part of the universal mediatorial order.

There is no idolatry in invoking the saints, for we do not invoke them as God, or gods, but simply as men, united with us in one and the same communion — not separated from us by death, but, in fact, brought nearer to us and rendered more able to assist us. There is no superstition in it, because we ask of the saints nothing that they are not able to give or competent to do. We ask only their prayers, and these they can give, are always willing to give; and their prayers, prompted by pure disinterested love, and having for their end the greater glory of God, must be well pleasing to their and our Lord.

There is nothing in this invocation derogatory to the honor of our Lord. Nothing is more pleasing to us than the honors paid to those we ourselves love and honor. And equally pleasing, therefore, must be to our Lord whatever love and honor we pay to the saints, who are His brothers, and whom He deigns to call His friends, for He in His humanity is man in all points as we are, sin excepted.[31] Nay,

---

[31] Cf. Heb. 4:15.

to refuse to honor them by our prayers would be a gross indignity, a grave affront, offered to Him. Especially is this true with regard to Mary, the Mother of God. Between our Lord and her there is the real relation of mother and son, as real in Heaven as it was on earth. Our Lord, as the Son of Mary, loves and honors her as His Mother, and always will do so. Judge, then, by your own love and reverence for your mother whether He can be jealous of the honors paid to His Mother; whether He must not Himself delight to load her with honors and to see all others honoring her.

So far from detracting from the honor due to God in invoking His saints, we honor Him in the most pleasing and delicate manner in our power by showing honor to them. It is to honor them that He permits them to intercede with Him for others, and, in soliciting them to intercede for us, we do only what He Himself does; we honor whom He honors, and the honor we render them is included in the reward He bestows on all who have followed Him in the regeneration.

There is, then, an evident fitness in the doctrine of saint worship as taught by the Church and practiced by her children. It harmonizes with the whole plan of creation and of redemption. And they little suspect how much they lose who neglect it, and what indignity they offer to God and His saints who willfully reject it — who treat as idolaters, debased and besotted by superstition, those who faithfully practice it, delighting to love and honor those whom God Himself loves and delights to honor.

Chapter Twelve

The Incarnation has exalted human nature

I have defended the invocation and intercession of the saints on the principle of mediation: the fact that God made all His creatures media in developing and perfecting His works — that is, in effecting their return to Him as their final cause, last end, or supreme beatitude. Does not this imply that the saints are mediators contrary to the assertion of St. Paul: "There is one God, and one mediator of God and men, the man Christ Jesus"?[32]

Strictly speaking, there *is* but one mediator, the man Christ Jesus. I neither overlook nor contradict this fact. Yet there is a sense in which the saints really share in the

[32] 1 Tim. 2:5.

glory of the mediatorial kingdom, although they mediate only in Christ and by virtue of their oneness with Him.

We have seen, as our Faith teaches, that God is Trinity. It is essential to the conception of God, as self-sufficing and self-existent being, being in its actuality and its plenitude, that He should contain in Himself, in His essence, His own principle, medium, and end — that is, should be indivisibly Triune. These three relations in the divine essence our Faith calls Father, Son, and Holy Spirit. To recall what has already been said: In creating the world, the whole Trinity concurs, each Person according to His respective relation to the others in the divine essence: the Father as principle; the Son, or Word, as medium; and the Holy Spirit as end, or consummation. In the second order, the return of existences to God as their last end, which is in some sense a new creation, and which our Lord Himself calls the regeneration, the three Persons of the Trinity alike concur, for God is one, and the distinction of Persons in no sense impairs the unity of His being; but they concur in diverse respects, as in the first order — the Father as principle, the Son as medium, and the Holy Spirit as end, or consummation, of the new creation.

But there is a remarkable difference between the first order, or procession, by way of creation, of existences from

God as first cause, and the second order, or return of existences, by way of regeneration, to God as last end, final cause, beatitude, supreme good. In the first order, the Son is the medium in His divinity alone, as the Eternal Word who was in the beginning, who was with God, and who is God.[33]

In the second order, however, the Son is the medium in His humanity, as the Word made flesh, as God become man. There is one God, and there is one mediator of God and men, the man Christ Jesus. So that, in the return of existences, in the regeneration, the creature is raised by the Hypostatic Union to the dignity of being the medium of his own redemption, regeneration, and final glorification.

In creation, God acts solely in His divinity, for creatures do not and cannot cooperate in their own production from nothing. God alone, in His own inherent, essential, and eternal divinity creates; but in regeneration, which presupposes creation, the creature is united hypostatically to the Word, and cooperates with the divinity, and shares in the glory of his own completion and return to God. This is the mystery of godliness, of the

[33]Cf. John 1:1.

Word manifested in the flesh,[34] which fills the angels with wonder and awe, and makes men tremble before the exalted destiny of their race and the glory and honor with which God, in His infinite love and infinite wisdom, crowns His creature man. In the regeneration, man is on the side of God, cooperates with Him, and shares in His honor and glory. What more can even the infinite God Himself do? And well may it be said that the Incarnation raises the creative act to its highest possible power, for in it the Creator makes the creature one with Himself.

The Incarnation is the assumption by the Word of human nature to be really, truly, hypostatically the nature of God. The Hypostatic Union, or the union of the divine and the human, is by the creative act of God alone, in which, as I have said, the whole Trinity concurs, as in every creative act of God; and in it the creature has no agency, in no sense cooperates, for it is God who assumes man, not man who assumes God. This act of union completes the first order and inaugurates the second. But in this second order, inaugurated or founded by the Incarnation, the creature enters integrally into the mediator, and is active and cooperative in the work of mediation (as follows

[34] 1 Tim. 3:16.

necessarily from the condemnation of the Monophysites, and Monothelites, who absorbed the human in the divine). The mediator of God and men is the man Christ Jesus, the creature hypostatically united to the Creator.

The man Christ Jesus holds the same relation to regenerated humanity that Adam holds to generated humanity, and hence, the apostle calls him the "second Adam."[35] He is the father of the human race in the order of regeneration, as Adam was in the order of generation. As no one can be a man, or pertain to the human race in the order of generation, unless born of Adam, so no one can be a man in the order of regeneration, or, what is the same thing, the order of grace, unless born again of Christ and made a new creature in Him. The birth from Adam is by natural generation and is therefore called natural birth, and the order of generation is commonly called the natural order, or simply nature. The birth from Christ, or the new birth in Him by the Holy Spirit, is spiritual, and by the election of grace. But it is as really a birth as natural birth, and as necessary in the order of return to God as is the natural birth in the order of the procession from God. Therefore, says our Lord to Nicodemus, "Unless a man be born again,

[35]Cf. 1 Cor. 15:45.

he cannot see the kingdom of God"[36] — cannot enter into the order of regeneration, far less attain to God as his last end, as the fulfillment of his destiny, or his supreme beatitude.

[36] Cf. John 3:5.

Chapter Thirteen

＊

The saints are mediators in Christ

Now, as all men in the natural order were in Adam, so in the order of grace, all are in Christ. All were in Adam generically, and potentially individualized in Him. We know this because generation is simply explication, not creation, and secondly, because all sinned in him and in him incurred the guilt of Original Sin, as Faith teaches us.

The Blessed Virgin, as of the race of Adam, must have incurred Original Sin generically in him, but she never incurred it individually or personally, because she was by special grace, or the anticipated application of the merits of Jesus Christ, preserved or exempted from it in the very first instant of her conception, so that she was conceived without original stain. And, therefore, her Immaculate Conception forms no exception to the fact that all of our race sinned in Adam. And if all sinned in him, all were in him.

But as all men in the order of generation were in Adam, so are all men in the order of regeneration in Christ, as is plainly implied by the apostle when he says, "As in Adam all die, so also in Christ all shall be made alive."[37] Entire human nature was assumed by the Word, for our Lord is perfect man as well as perfect God. He assumed humanity, which was individualized in Him as it was in Adam, and hence, He is in the order of regeneration "the head of every man"[38] — nay, the head of every creature; for the whole lower creation, being made for man, is regenerated and returns to God in man. That all are included in Him, as included in the humanity He assumed, is affirmed by the fact that He died for all and made ample satisfaction or atonement for all. But He made atonement for men only as their head, and the Passion and Cross avail us only as we suffer them in Him, as His members. There is nothing fictitious or unreal in the gospel, and nothing is counted so which is not really so. To live with Christ, we must suffer with Him, and to be

[37] 1 Cor. 15:22.
[38] 1 Cor. 11:3.

practically benefitted by His Passion and Cross, we must endure them in Him. And that we cannot do unless we are in Him. He redeems, elevates, and restores humanity, because He *is* humanity, and in Him humanity is obedient unto death, even the death of the Cross.[39] If all were not included in the human nature assumed, the obedience of Christ could not have sufficed for all, for we can no more obey in Christ if we are not in Him than we could sin in Adam if we were not in Adam. The humanity taken by the Word was as broad, as full, and as entire as the humanity of Adam.

Now, as the Son of God is the mediator of God and men in His human nature, and as the saints are included in that human nature, as all men were included in Adam, they certainly are included in the mediator, and therefore are, in a certain sense, mediators; for they only with Him constitute what St. Augustine calls the *Totus Christus*.[40]

[39] Phil. 2:8.

[40] Brownson here repeats the teaching that the baptized who profess the truth bequeathed by Christ and are subject to those appointed by Him to rule the Church are brought into most intimate union with Him. Each individual, although living his own life and having his own responsibilities and concerns, is joined to Christ and receives the life of sanctifying grace from Him, as the

Yet they are mediators in Him as all men are sinners in Adam, not personally, but generically. Entire humanity was redeemed, regenerated, and glorified in Christ — and entire creation also, as included in man — and was in Him, or rather, He in it, the medium of redemption, regeneration, and glorification — but generically, not individually, as all men were included generically, not individually, in Adam. In the natural order, the explication of individuals is necessary and takes place, we have seen, by natural generation. In the order of regeneration, it does not take place in that way (for in that order, "they neither marry nor are given in marriage"[41]), but, as I have said, by grace, and they are individually or personally born into that order by the election of grace. But the explication is as real

cells, nerves, and organs of a human body depend on the head. This truth has been concretized by the term "the Mystical Body of Christ." In this sense, not only the saints in Heaven, but also the just on earth, in a secondary and subordinate manner, are mediators with Christ. Thus, St. Augustine, following St. Paul's words to the Corinthians, "Now you are the body of Christ, member for member" (cf. 1 Cor. 12:27), used the term "the Whole Christ" to indicate, not only the Lord in Himself, but as including all — the just on earth and the blessed in Heaven — who are joined to Him. — ED.

[41]Cf. Matt. 22:30.

and as necessary by grace as the explication of individuals by natural regeneration. This is why we do not call the saints personally or individually mediators, in the strict and absolute sense of the term. They mediate, not personally, individually, in their own independent right, but in Christ, as included generically in His human nature.

Yet as in neither order is the individual ever without the race, or the race without the individual, the saints, who are individual explications by grace of the human nature assumed by Christ, and as they have their origin and root in that nature, really do, in a relative and secondary sense, perform a share in the mediatorial work of our Lord, not indeed as first cause, but as second causes. If they did not in some sense share with Christ in His mediatorial work, how could He say to them, "Well done, good and faithful servants; enter into the joy of your Lord"?[42] How could He promise them Heaven as a *reward*? Can He fail in His promises? Or can He reward men for doing what they have not done? Men are not, as the apostle James says, justified by faith alone;[43] and the condemnation of the reformers is that they denied — in denying the merit

[42] Cf. Matt. 25:21, 23.
[43] James 2:24.

of good works, and asserting justification by faith alone, and conversion, or regeneration, by the direct and immediate act of the Holy Spirit — the whole mediatorial system revealed to us in the gospel. Perhaps we are all a little too afraid of asserting in sufficiently strong terms the agency of the creature in the second order, and too prone in our feelings of reverence to separate Christ too widely from His saints, and to isolate the humanity He assumed from our common humanity. We cannot use too strong terms to express the intimacy between Him and the saints, or conceive a closer relation than really exists between His human nature and our own.

I think I have said enough to show that the objection has no force, that it either urges nothing that may not be conceded, or rests on a false principle and a total misapprehension of the real Catholic doctrine of mediation. We cannot place the saints higher than God places them; we cannot give them higher honor than He gives them; and in no possible way can we exaggerate their merits. We cannot, unless we confound them with the divinity, give them too high a worship, or offer them a worship that detracts from that due to God Himself.

Chapter Fourteen

The Communion of Saints unites us with the blessed in Heaven

In the regeneration, what may be called the order of the end, which is founded by the Incarnation, and in which creation is completed and man finds his supreme good by being supernaturally united to the Supreme Good Himself, the paternal and filial relations are spiritual, but no less real than in the order of generation commencing with Adam. Our spiritual fathers are no less real fathers than our fathers after the flesh. Priests are called fathers and really are so. And as fathers of our spiritual life, they are fathers of a higher order and in a higher sense than our natural fathers — as much higher as the life of the soul is above the life of the body. Perhaps in this fact is at least one of the reasons the Church insists on the celibacy of the clergy. There would be a sort of bigamy in it, for the priest is wedded to the Church, his true spouse and our spiritual mother. The new birth is as really a birth as natural birth, and the priest married in the natural order seems to be a priest of the order of Aaron, rather than a priest of the order of Melchisedech. The spiritual father owes all his love, all his care and tenderness, to his spiritual children and ought not to be burdened with children after the flesh.

They who object to the celibacy of the clergy may find here an answer to their objections. The priest is not really a celibate. He has a spiritual bride and spiritual children, who develop in him all the higher and nobler qualities of the husband and father. Nor are those virgins who reject marriage after the flesh, and take the vow of chastity, less really wives and mothers than are wives and mothers in the natural order. They are espoused in the spiritual order, and to each may be applied the words of Scripture: "He who has become your husband is your Maker."[44] They are mothers, and "many are the children of the desolate, more than of her that hath a husband."[45]

[44]Cf. Isa. 54:5.
[45]Isa. 54:1; Gal. 4:27.

In this cold and material age, we are prone to regard only the material as real, and only the flesh as living, and to treat what is spiritual as unreal, illusory, imaginary. Hence, this spiritual espousal and this spiritual maternity is regarded as a device to cheat the mind and take captive the imagination by words without meaning. We remain in the order of generation, and although we profess to have faith, we appear not to have been initiated into the order of regeneration; we appear hardly to believe that there is such an order. And yet our Lord said, "Mary hath chosen the best part."[46] Have we yet to learn that the end of generation is regeneration, and that the real significance of the material is in the spiritual? Have we failed to penetrate the great mystery or sacrament of which St. Paul speaks, and to understand that marriage and maternity in the natural order are symbolic of the higher and more real marriage and maternity?

If the blessed Mary held to us only a purely spiritual relation, she would be really our mother, holding to us, in the order of regeneration, the relation held to us by Eve in the order of generation — the mother of our spiritual life, as Eve was the mother of our natural life. It is so that the

[46]Luke 10:42.

Fathers regard her. They call her the second Eve, through whom life comes into the world, as death came through the first Eve; by whom we gain more than we lost by our mother in the order of the flesh. In this sense alone, Mary would be a real mother of the regenerated, the seat of wisdom, cause of our joy, and gate of Heaven.

But she is our mother in a sense more tangible to those who have difficulty in accepting spiritual relations as real. I have shown that, through the Incarnation, the regenerated are joined to God by identity of nature and are, so to speak, the natural brothers of our Lord; and therefore His Mother must be really our mother. He took His flesh from her, and she was as truly His Mother as any mother is the mother of her own son. She thus became literally the mother of regenerated humanity, as Eve was the mother of humanity in the order of generation.

I say *regenerated humanity*, because the human nature assumed by our Lord was not assumed with its own personality (which would have been adoptionism) and because, by the very fact of assumption, it was regenerated and elevated to its highest possible degree. As we are not born into the regeneration by natural generation, but by grace infused by the Holy Spirit, only they can really claim Mary for their mother who are born again, and thus so connected, not only with natural humanity, as they are through Eve, but with regenerated humanity, of which Mary is really and truly the mother. Of all others, she is only potentially, not actually, the mother; as our Lord Himself — although He died for all men and made ample satisfaction for all, and therefore is potentially the Redeemer and Savior of all men — is actually the Redeemer only of the regenerated, and actually the Savior only of the elect.

All, then, who have been regenerated, born anew as begotten by the Holy Spirit, have the right to call Mary *mother,* and our Lord Himself *Brother.* Only in our Lord, the human nature is completed, its destiny attained, while in us, it is in its infancy, for we have not yet attained — and as long as we are in the flesh, we shall not have attained — to the stature of perfect men in Christ Jesus.[47] Therefore is He called our elder Brother, our Forerunner, who has already entered in, while we remain without, awaiting His intercession for us. All of us who are born again in Baptism, the sacrament of regeneration, and who love our Lord Jesus Christ are really and truly children of Mary, and she is really and truly our mother.

[47] Cf. Eph. 4:13.

Saint Worship and the Worship of Mary

She *is* our mother, for it is the blessed privilege of us who believe in life eternal and the Communion of Saints to regard the holy ones in Heaven as living and present with us. We see them, not with the eyes of the body, but with the eye of faith. We embrace them, not with our bodily arms, but with our love, and are embraced by them with their love. They are present to our hearts, and we can speak to them, pour into their open and sympathizing hearts our joys and griefs, and ask and receive their aid, as readily and as effectually as when they were present to our bodily senses. They have not departed from us, have not deserted us and left us desolate. Death has not removed them from us, and there is no need of evocation or necromancy to enjoy their communion, to obtain their advice or their help. Were all that the spiritists pretend a fact, instead of being, as it is, of the enemy of souls, it would fall immeasurably short of the blessed communion every true follower of Christ has with the blessed in Heaven. Why can we not learn that the unseen and invisible is more real than the seen and visible?

I have dwelt on this point to show that the warm expressions of Catholic piety in reference to Mary, the Mother of God, rarely, if ever, exceed the sober truth. Even the expressions that many Catholics regard as exaggerations fall short of the reality — and I doubt exaggeration is possible. What I have said vindicates most thoroughly from the charge of enthusiasm, superstition, or visionariness those admirable associations of children of Mary in our parishes, colleges, and academies, and also the efforts of earnest priests and devout women to extend and intensify devotion to Mary, as the Mother of God, and as our own dear and loving mother. They are grateful to the nobler and richer sentiments of our hearts, tend to honor her whom God honored above all women in choosing her to be His Mother, and serve to keep fresh and living in our souls faith in the Incarnation, on which all our hopes of Heaven, and even of civilization, depend.

Chapter Fifteen

⌐

We are permitted
to honor holy images

"Is it allowable to honor relics, crucifixes, and holy pictures?
Yes, with an inferior and relative honor, as related to
Christ and His saints, and as memorials of them. *May we
then pray to relics and images? No,* by no means, for they
have no life, or sense, to hear or help us."

So says the catechism, and so the Catholic Church
teaches all her children. Relics of saints, crucifixes, holy
pictures, and images may be honored with an inferior and
relative honor, because they are related to our Lord and
His saints, and are memorials of them, and serve to keep
them fresh in our memories. And why should they not be
honored? When one is thought to be dying, far from
home, among strangers, some dear old lady who had been

kind to him cuts off a lock of his hair to send to his mother. The lover wears the portrait of his beloved next to his heart, and prizes everything that has belonged to her. The pious son preserves with tender care the picture of his mother and will not suffer it to be profaned. The mother preserves the playthings and little coat of her infant boy when his body sleeps in the churchyard, or cherishes with almost painful fondness every memorial of her heroic son slain on the battlefield fighting for his country. Is the saint, the martyr slain, fighting for that nobler country, Heaven, the true *patria* of the soul, less dear to the memory of the Christian heart?

The republic delights to honor her patriotic sons, those who have fallen in her cause, who have defended her in danger, led her armies to victory, secured her independence, or rendered her illustrious by their statesmanship. She erects monuments to show her deep sense of their worth and to perpetuate the memory of their civic virtues. Do we not call the national capital Washington, and does not a picture of "the Father of our Country" hang in many a buildling in America? Does not the nation preserve among its choicest treasures the very coat and sword he wore? Is there a state in the Union that has not a Washington county, city, or village, or a city that has not a Washington Street? Has not a national association of noble-minded and noble-hearted women purchased for the nation the land on which stands his tomb,[48] that it may, through all time, be free to the pilgrimage of the grateful sons and daughters of the republic that he had the chief hand in founding? The same honors in kind, although less in degree, are paid to others who have given luster to the nation by their genius, their talents, and their public services.

The Church has her battles and religion her victories. Should they who battled for the Church, gained through grace the victory for religion, and came off conquerors, and more than conquerors, be regarded as less deserving of honor? Is there a greater or truer hero than the Christian hero, than he who gives up all for Jesus and never ceases to do valiant battle against all His enemies? Our Lord judges not so, for to such a one He promises a crown of life, of immortal glory and honor, in His kingdom. The civil hero

[48]In 1858, when Mount Vernon had fallen into a state of disrepair, Miss Ann Pamela Cunningham organized the Mount Vernon Ladies' Association, which purchased the mansion and land and restored the estate. The association still preserves the house and the tomb of the first president. — ED.

must add the Christian virtues to his civil virtues, or fail of the heavenly glory. Why, then, should relics, pictures, statues, and memorials of a saint be less deserving of honor than those of a mother, a sweetheart, or a patriot?

The principle on which rests the veneration of relics, crucifixes, and holy pictures is natural and dear to the human heart, and I have shown, over and over again, as the Church teaches, that grace does not supersede nature. Most true is it that nature is below the plane of our origin and end, for they are both supernatural, and we can do nothing without the regenerating grace of Jesus Christ to gain or merit eternal life. But grace supposes nature, accepts, elevates, purifies, and directs it. Whatever is true and beautiful in nature or natural affection Christianity hallows and makes her own.

When I ask a saint to pray for me, I am guilty of no superstition, for I ask only what he can do. But if I ask him to raise, or if I believe he can raise, a dead body to life, I fall into gross superstition, because that only God can do. God may raise the dead to life in answer to the prayer of the saint, but no saint, not even our blessed Lady, can do it. When I honor relics, crucifixes, holy pictures, and images only as memorials of Christ and His saints, reverence them only as related to the real worth I venerate, I am neither superstitious nor an idolater. I simply treat things as they are, and for what they are. I simply adhere to truth.

"But the practice of Catholics is forbidden by the Decalogue." I think not. God does not forbid in one law what He authorizes in another. What is forbidden in what Catholics call the First Commandment, and Protestants the First and Second, is the making, keeping, or honoring of pictures, not as memorials, but as gods. "I am the Lord thy God, who brought thee out of the land of Egypt, out of the house of bondage. Thou shalt not have strange gods before me. Thou shalt not make to thyself a graven thing, nor the likeness of anything that is in heaven above, or in the earth beneath, nor of those things that are in the waters under the earth. *Thou shalt not adore them, nor serve them.*"[49] It is plain that what is here forbidden is neither painting nor sculpture, but the making of images to be worshiped and served as gods. Otherwise everyone who has his likeness rendered by either the painter or the sculptor would break the precept. The great gentile apostasy had taken place prior to Moses, and idolatry had become very general in his time. It was one of the main purposes of the Hebrew sacred law to protect the Hebrew

[49]Exod. 20:2-5.

people from the infection of the prevailing worship of false gods and to keep alive with them the knowledge and worship of the one living and true God. Many things were, no doubt, prohibited to them that otherwise might have been allowed, but it cannot be supposed that Moses understood the prohibition in the rigid Protestant and Islamic sense, for he himself ordered the construction of the brazen image of a serpent, and of the cherubim whose outstretched wings over the ark covered the mercy-seat;[50] nor did the Jews understand it in that sense, for the gold sea in their Temple rested on twelve brazen oxen.[51] Evidently the precept is directed against idolatry, the worship of false gods, not against the arts of painting and sculpture.

Moreover, the heathen themselves, as I understand it, did not worship literally that which they believed or knew to be made with men's hands. What, in their own minds, they worshiped was the demon or numen that they believed entered into the image upon the sacerdotal consecration or conjuration, and afterward dwelt therein. But as this belief was vain, and the numen or demon supposed to inhabit the image was also vain, the sacred writers, who

[50]Num. 21:9; Exod. 25:18, 22.
[51]Cf. 4 Kings 16:17 (RSV = 2 Kings 16:17).

treat things as they really are, without taking notice of what is purely subjective, represent the heathen as literally worshiping gods of wood and stone fashioned by men's hands, because there was, objectively, nothing else present to be worshiped. As no Christian believes that God, whom the heaven of heavens cannot contain, or that even a saint, can be shut up in an image made by human hands, or confounds the image with that which it represents, no Christian can, in keeping and honoring holy pictures and images, be in the least danger of falling into the sin of the heathen, or be regarded as violating the precept.

≈

Chapter Sixteen

Relics and holy images
keep the Faith alive in our hearts

That the honor we pay to relics, crucifixes, sacred pictures, and images might, while Greek and Roman idolatry was predominant in the empire, have been taken in a superstitious or idolatrous sense by some only half-converted from heathenism and have led the heathen to regard Christians themselves as idolaters, is not impossible. It would seem that, while the danger of awakening old idolatrous or superstitious associations remained, these memorials, although carefully preserved, were exhibited with more reserve to the reverence of the faithful than after Christianity had taken possession of the empire, and the discipline of the secret *disciplina arcani* was no longer necessary or even practicable.

Saint Worship and the Worship of Mary

The use of images did not originate idolatry with the heathen. The culpable loss or corruption of the knowledge of God preceded the idolatrous worship of images, or the worship as gods of things that are not God. The Gentiles had the knowledge of the true God, but "when they knew God, they have not glorified Him as God, or given thanks; but became vain in their thoughts; and their foolish heart was darkened. For, professing themselves to be wise, they became fools. And they changed the glory of the incorruptible God into the likeness of the image of a corruptible man, and of birds, and of four-footed beasts, and of creeping things."[52] But while men retain uncorrupted the knowledge of the true God, they cannot confound Him with anything visible — with the sun or moon or stars — far less with an image that man has painted or carved.

Memorials of our Lord and the saints, so far from tending to obscure that knowledge in the minds or hearts of the faithful, have the contrary effect: that of tending to keep it more clear, fresh, and living in the heart. Nothing can tend more directly to bring home the great facts of the Incarnation and the Redemption, on which all our hopes

[52]Rom. 1:21-23.

of salvation depend, than to kneel before the image of Christ dying on the Cross for us. The son does not forget his mother in contemplating her picture, or the lover his beloved. The patriot does not find his knowledge of Washington obscured, or his love for him or his country weakened, by looking on Washington's coat or sword, which the nation preserves. Everybody knows and feels that the contrary is the fact. Experience proves that they who object to the relative honor that Catholics pay to the memorials of Christ and His saints as superstitious or idolatrous gradually lose the sense of the Incarnation and are by no means remarkable for their knowledge and love of the saints and martyrs. Yet they also, with an inconsistency that does them honor, cherish such memorials as they have of the reformers, who are their saints and great men. There is preserved in the Watburg even yet, I am told, the inkstand that Luther threw in the Devil's face, and pilgrims are shown the black spot it left on the wall.

But it is said that these memorials are addressed to the senses and can only tend to give our piety an outward, sensible character and prevent the mind from turning inward and becoming acquainted with the deeper, internal spiritual life. The contrary is the fact. These memorials direct the mind at once to the spiritual life, for they are nothing to the Catholic save as memorials of such life, external symbols of the interior and spiritual. Perhaps they are not such to the Protestant, who has no acquaintance with the deeper spiritual life familiar to every saint, and in some degree to every Catholic.

Do not be scandalized, my dear Protestant friend. There are more things in Heaven and on earth than are dreamt of in your philosophy or attained in your pious meditations. Our Catholic worship seems to you external, sensual, and unspiritual, because you have in your own spiritual experience no key that unlocks its mysterious depths. These memorials, so dear and significant to us Catholics, so powerful to place us in the presence of God, and to make us feel that we belong to the Communion of Saints, are to you no memorials at all and tell you nothing beyond what they are in themselves. But is that our fault?

Then again, it must not be forgotten that the living man is body and soul united, not body alone, nor soul alone, and the senses in their place and in their proper use are as essential to man as the intellect. Man is not a pure intelligence and grasps the intelligible only as sensibly represented. He can no more live and act without sense than without reason. For him, pure spiritualism is as impossible as pure sensism. Hence, the principle and reason of external worship. A purely internal worship is as insuf-ficient as a purely external worship, and experience proves that they who reject all external worship soon come to neglect all internal. Worship demands the homage of our whole man. Christianity elevates, purifies, and directs our nature, but rejects no part of it. The whole is from God and should be returned to Him as His due. In all true religion, there is indeed a mystical element, but they who seek to be pure mystics, to live in this world as pure, disembodied spirits, mistake the nature of religion and the capabilities of man. Memorials of Christ and His saints help us precisely because, like music and speech, they are external signs and are addressed to our senses, conveying a truth, a spiritual reality, to the understanding and the heart.

But in the relics of the saints, we are told by men who esteem themselves wise, Catholics worship dead men's flesh and bones, rottenness and corruption. We do not *worship* the relics of saints, in the sense the objectors mean. But the objection shows how far the age that brings it has departed from the true sense of the Incarnation and the Christian doctrine of the Resurrection. The Christian does not view these relics as do those who lack the Chris-tian's faith and the Christian's hope. This flesh and these bones have been redeemed by our Lord, for He assumed flesh, took upon Himself a real human body, not simply a human soul. And in assuming a human body, He redeemed all material nature, all the elements of which are included in the human body (whence the ancients term man a *microcosm*, or world in little). In the Incarnation, all material nature has been assumed and purified, and "Holy to the Lord," as foretold by the prophet, has been written on everything. Hence, Peter, in a vision, was forbidden to call any creature common or unclean.[53] The relics of the saint have also been cleansed and sanctified by the prayers, vigils, fasts, mortifications, and holy life of the saint — purified and sanctified by the grace of God, so freely bestowed on the saint, and so fully complied with by him.

Moreover, these relics are not the flesh and bones of dead men. The saints are not dead; they live, and live in Heaven, in the presence of God, and enjoy the glory of their Lord. Have we forgotten that life and immortality are brought to light through the gospel? And is the future life only a hope and not a reality to men calling themselves Christians, as it was and is to the heathen? But

[53] Acts 10:28.

more than this the Christian knows: not only does the soul live, but this very flesh which once clothed the saint shall rise again and live forever, for does not the Christian sing with the Church, "I believe in the resurrection of the body"? Hence, even our bodies should be sanctified and preserved pure, for they are destined to rise again, to an immortal life.

The honor the Church pays to the relics of saints and martyrs is an honor due them as related to our Lord Himself through His assumption of flesh, and as having in some sense shared in the holy life and sanctity of the saint. But it serves also to keep alive in our minds and fresh in our hearts the great and glorious article of our Faith, the resurrection of the body.

This said, the reason for honoring with an inferior and relative honor, as expressed in the catechism, pictures and statues of the saints, as well as of our Lord in His humanity, is obvious. They are related to the saints in an inferior degree, but still related to them and, although feebler than relics, are yet memorials of them, which keep alive in us the great Catholic principles and virtues the saints honored in their lives and direct us to that Fountain of Grace whence they drew the strength to come off conquerors in the battle of life.

☙

Chapter Seventeen

Saint worship deepens our faith

In these pages, which I now conclude, my object has been, not to eulogize the saints, nor to say what has been said and better said a hundred times before, nor yet to exhibit my own devotion to the saints or belief in the pious legends that circulate among the faithful; but to show, in the clearest and simplest manner I could, the principles on which the *cultus sanctorum* rests, and their relation alike to the principles of the natural order and to those which underlie all the great mysteries of the Christian revelation.

I have written on the assumption that all principles are catholic, and all truth is one, and therefore what is true in nature is true in grace; and that, although grace is above nature, elevating and completing it, it is in no wise contradictory to nature or disconnected with it. One and the same dialectic principle runs through all the Creator's works, for all have their archetype in His own indivisible and triune essence, and all are parts of one indissoluble whole, in the divine mind already completed and brought into perfect union with Him. Hence, while I distinguish creation from the Creator, as the act is distinguished from the actor, I do not separate it from God. I distinguish between nature and grace, but do not separate in the regenerate the one from the other, for both proceed alike from God, and both are alike necessary to the life and perfection of man, or the fulfillment of the divine purpose in his creation.

I have been so intent on showing the connection of grace with nature, and setting forth the rational element of the Christian mysteries in general, and of saint worship in particular, that some readers may have thought me disposed to rationalize too much. But I have never forgotten that our Faith contains mysteries beyond the reach of reason either to discover or to explain, which every believer receives on faith in God revealing and in the Church proposing. I have simply aimed at developing the principle contained in the direction of our Lord when He bids us "consider the lilies of the field" and "behold the birds of the air."[54] Our Lord often conveys His instructions by analogies and illustrations borrowed from the natural world, which would not be possible if nature had no analogy with grace or with the revealed mysteries. I have done what I could to seize these natural analogies, to illustrate and defend by them the worship we Catholics render to the saints.

On the other hand, I have aimed to show the reason and propriety of this worship in the admitted mysteries of our Faith itself and to demonstrate that it flows logically from the great mysteries of creation and Incarnation. We worship God in His works because He enters and remains in them by His creative act. We worship God in His humanity because, by His assumption of human nature, He has made it henceforth and forever His own nature and inseparable in our worship from His divine nature. We reverence His saints for their imitation, through grace, of His merits; their union, through regeneration, with Him; and their inseparability from Him in glory. We could not render Him a full and complete worship if we excluded His saints, for they make but one with Him and are included in the *totus Christus*, as St. Augustine teaches. Nor

[54]Matt. 6:26, 28.

could we give full expression to our love of Him if we did not suffer it to extend to all that He loves or that is in any way related to Him.

Moreover, as in the Incarnation, our Lord assumed flesh, a real body, and as in the human body are all the elements of the lower creation, He has by His assumption united all material nature to Himself as final cause, as in creation all are united to Him as first cause, so that God is all and in all. And all lower orders of creation, since all proceed from God for man and return to Him in man, are sacred and entitled in their degree to share in the honor we owe to God in His humanity.

I have endeavored also to show that the worship of the saints is the best practical protection of the faithful against the errors of atheism, pantheism, and idolatry, and the best means to keep fresh in their minds and hearts faith in all the great mysteries of Christian revelation. All the practices authorized by the Church are dictated by Christian dogmas and preserve them in our Faith by realizing them in our lives. No one who has devotion to Mary can forget the Incarnation and what depends on it. No one who prays to a saint can doubt the future life or regard the joys of Heaven as a poetic dream. No one who honors the relics of a great servant of God can hesitate about believing in the resurrection of the body. There is a remarkable proof of this in the fact that all the sects that reject the worship of Mary and of the saints, and sneer at sacred relics, crucifixes, and pictures and statues of our Lord and His saints invariably lose, step by step, their faith in the Christian mysteries and fall into naked rationalism, or a vague sentimentalism that depends on no dogma and respects no dogmatic teaching. The Church teaches us our Faith and preserves it by training us to live it, and hence, the great masters of spiritual life have always considered a tender devotion to Mary and the saints as a sign of election, and the want of it as an unfavorable symptom.

I have endeavored to express myself in clear and intelligible language and, as far as I could, in exact language. But I have intentionally avoided the phraseology usually adopted, because I think that it has become in some respects routine, and hundreds and thousands read it without once seriously asking themselves what it really means; and also because non-Catholics have read or heard attached to it a false and erroneous sense, which has prejudiced them against us, and I have wished to use language that would not mislead them, but in fact convey to their minds our real meaning. It has been thought by some that

Saint Worship and the Worship of Mary

I have failed in this respect by using the word *worship*. In the restricted sense of the word commonly adopted, we do not *worship* Mary or the saints, but that restricted sense is not its only or its leading sense, and I have been unable to find any other English word that fully expresses what is meant by *cultus* in Latin. I explained at the outset the sense in which I have used it, a proper sense, for worship is of various kinds and degrees, and no intelligent reader can for a moment suppose that I mean that we worship the saint with the same worship that we give to God.

If my words have been profitable to no others, their preparation has been profitable to me and has given me much peace and serenity of mind, quickened my love of Mary and of the saints of our Lord, and rendered dearer both the Catholic Faith and Catholic worship. I bless God for the Communion of Saints and beg them to pray for me, that I may not be lost.

Part II

The Worship of Mary

~

Chapter Eighteen

We offer Mary a higher worship than we offer the saints

We worship Mary, not only as St. Mary, in common with all the saints; we render her also a special and much higher worship. This worship is authorized by her unique relation to the mystery of the Incarnation, and therefore to our salvation, and is rendered in honor of that mystery itself; that is, in honor of God in His human as well as His divine nature. Those who reject the Incarnation can understand nothing of this worship and have no lot or part in it, for they can neither worship God in His human nature, nor admit that He really assumed flesh from the flesh of Mary. To them Mary is only an ordinary woman and holds no special relation to the mystery of redemption. She has, in their view, nothing to do with our salvation and is related to the faithful just like any other woman. They assign her no special position or office in the economy of God's gracious providence. They are offended when they hear us call her the Mother of God and sneer at us when they hear us address her as our own dear mother. We have nothing here to say to them. The worship of Mary presupposes the Incarnation, and they who shrink from it show by that fact that they do not really believe in the mystery, and therefore do not really embrace the Christian religion, and at best make only a hollow profession of it. There is and can be no truer test of one's active, living faith in our holy religion, in the redemption and salvation of sinners through the Cross, than a firm attachment to the worship of Mary. This is probably why devotion to Mary is commonly regarded by the saints as a sign of election.

The particular honor we render to Mary, called by our writers *hyperdulia* — as distinguished from simple *dulia,* or the worship we pay to all the saints — presupposes the real Incarnation of our Lord in her chaste womb, and her real and subsisting maternal relation to God made man. If you concede the Incarnation, you must concede that Mary is the Mother of God. If you deny that she is the Mother of God, you must deny the Incarnation. There is no middle course possible. If Mary is the mother of her Son, then the relations between mother and son and all that those relations imply subsist and must forever subsist between them, and she must be honored as the Mother of God, and therefore of grace, the grace through which we are redeemed and saved.

In the Incarnation, God becomes man without ceasing to be God and so assumes human nature that He becomes from the moment of the Incarnation as truly human as He is divine — perfect man as well as perfect God. It is not that a perfect man is united to perfect God, but that perfect God becomes Himself really perfect man, in such sort that the human nature is as truly the nature of the divine Person, or Word, as is the divine nature itself. The two natures are united in one Person, or the one Person is the hypostasis or the one *suppositum* of two distinct natures, one divine, the other human.

The tendency of Protestants, even of those who profess to hold the mystery of the Incarnation, is to regard the union, not as the union of two natures in one person, but as a simple moral union of two persons, one human, the other God. Hence, Protestants have a tendency to "dissolve Jesus" and to cherish the spirit of what the apostle St. John calls Antichrist. But the true doctrine of the

Incarnation, which we must admit if we admit any real Incarnation at all, is that the human and divine natures are united, without being confounded, in one divine Person. Person is distinguishable, but not separable, from nature, for no person is conceivable as really existing without a nature; and although human as well as divine nature is distinguishable from person, neither is conceivable as really existing without person or personality. The human nature of Christ is not human nature divested of personality; it is united to a person as much as is the human nature of Peter or John, but its Person is divine, not human — the eternal Person of the divine nature of Christ. Hence, Christ is two distinct natures in one Person, which divine Person is God, the second Person of the ever-adorable Trinity.

Now, God in His human nature is literally and truly the Son of Mary. She is not the mother of a human son received into union with God — the error of the Adoptionists, implying that the human nature of Christ has a human personality, which it has not and never had. Yet human nature cannot exist without a personality. So that which was conceived in the womb of Mary and born of her was the divine Person assuming to Himself flesh, or the nature of man, and was therefore God. Hence, in the strictest sense of the word, Mary is the Mother of God, and therefore God is as truly her Son as anyone is the son of his own mother.

Unquestionably, Mary was not the Mother of God in His divine nature, that is, the mother of the divinity, for in that sense God is eternal, necessary, and self-existent being, and the Creator of Mary, not her son. But God incarnate is still God, and God having assumed flesh is no less God in His human nature than in His divine nature. And therefore, Mary is nonetheless the Mother of God because she is His mother only in His human nature, for the human nature of which she is the mother is the human nature of God. She is not the mother of the divinity, but she is the Mother of God, for since the Incarnation, God the Son is the one Person of both divine nature and human nature, and is, as to nature, at once God and man.

How God can descend to be the Person of human nature, or exalt human nature to be truly His own, is a mystery we do not attempt to explain, which transcends every created intelligence, and which none but God Himself can fully comprehend. All we know or claim to know is that He has done so and thus, although our Creator, has become our Brother, flesh of our flesh, that we might be made partakers of His divine nature and live forever in a true society with Him.

Now, Mary, as the Mother of God, is something more than an ordinary woman and holds a place in the economy of grace different from that of any other woman, different from and above that of any other creature. She has been honored by the Creator as no other creature has been, for she alone has been selected by Him to be His Mother. If God has distinguished her from all other women, if He has chosen her to be His Mother, shall not we distinguish her from all other women, and honor her as His mother? What higher honor could God confer on a creature than He has conferred on Mary? Shall we not honor her whom God Himself delights to honor and, like Him, give her the highest honor we can give to a creature? We are to love and honor the Son as we love and honor the Father, and we are to love and honor Him in His humanity no less than in His divinity.

We cannot dissolve Christ. "Every spirit that dissolveth Jesus," says the blessed apostle John, "is not of God; and this is Antichrist, of whom you have heard that he cometh; and he is now already in the world."[55] We cannot dissolve

[55] 1 John 4:3.

Christ, and worship Him in His divine nature only, and refuse to worship Him in His human nature. He is one Christ — not two: one human, the other divine. He is two forever distinct natures in one Person, to be loved and honored alike in both natures, and therefore in her from whom He took His human nature. We cannot honor Him without honoring her, if we try, nor honor her as His Mother without honoring Him. Such is the intimate relation between the Mother and the Son that whatever honor we render her as His Mother redounds to Him, and whatever honor we render to Him as her Son — that is, to Him as come in the flesh — will overflow and extend to her. The two cannot be separated, for the flesh of the Son is of the flesh of the Mother; both have one and the same nature, and it is impossible to honor the nature in the one without honoring it in the other.

If we bear this in mind, we shall find no difficulty in justifying the peculiar worship of Mary or in vindicating the strongest language that Catholic piety has ever used in addressing her. Mary is the Mother of God; from her the Son of God took His flesh, His human nature. By this fact, she becomes intimately connected with the mystery of our redemption and final salvation. We are redeemed only by God, not in His divine nature, but in that very nature which He took from the womb of Mary. In the present providence of God, man could not be saved and be enabled to gain His supernatural end without the Incarnation of the Son. That is to say, man could be redeemed only by God in the flesh — God in human nature — for as the divine nature can neither suffer, nor obey, nor merit, it was only in human nature, in the flesh become really His nature, that God could perform the work of redemption, that He could satisfy for sin and merit for us the grace of pardon and sanctification. Mary is thus called, and rightly called, the Mother of Grace, for she is that inasmuch as she is mother of the sacred flesh through which grace has been purchased and is communicated to us.

Chapter Nineteen

We honor Mary's free consent to God's will

But God did not become incarnate in the womb of Mary without her free, voluntary consent. Thus, she, by her own will, cooperates in the work of our redemption, and therefore, for another reason, may be called the Mother of Grace and associated with our salvation. Much of what is said of Mary in this respect rests on the fact of this consent.

We might reasonably presume, from what we know of the dealings of God with men, that this consent was first obtained, for we could not well suppose that God would do violence to one He so loved as to choose her to be His Mother, or that He would be conceived in her womb against or without her free consent. It is evident also, from the history given us by St. Luke of the Annunciation, that this consent was asked and obtained:

> The angel Gabriel was sent from God into a city of Galilee called Nazareth, to a virgin espoused to a man whose name was Joseph, of the house of David; and the virgin's name was Mary. And the angel, being come in, said unto her: "Hail, full of grace, the Lord is with thee; blessed art thou among women." Who, having heard, was troubled at his saying, and thought with herself what manner of salutation this should be. And the angel said to her: "Fear not, Mary, for thou hast found grace with God. Behold, thou shalt conceive in thy womb and shalt bring forth a Son; and thou shalt call His name Jesus. He shall be great, and shall be called the Son of the Most High. And the Lord God shall give unto Him the throne of David His father; and He shall reign in the house of Jacob forever. And of His kingdom there shall be no end." And Mary said to the angel: "How shall this be done, because I know not man?" And the angel, answering, said to her: "The Holy Ghost shall come upon thee, and the power of the Most High shall overshadow thee.

And therefore also the Holy which shall be born of thee shall be called the Son of God. And behold, thy cousin Elizabeth, she also hath conceived a son in her old age; and this is the sixth month with her that is called barren. Because no word shall be impossible with God." And Mary said: *"Behold the handmaid of the Lord; be it done to me according to thy word."* And the angel departed from her.[56]

Here, manifestly, is consent asked and consent given, and although given, not given until an explanation has been demanded and received. It is plain from the narrative that Mary is not only a virgin, but is resolved always to be a virgin, and she does not give her consent until assured by the angel that she can become the mother of the Son of God without prejudice to her virginity. She knows not and will not know man, but when assured that this is not necessary, and referred to the conception of her cousin Elizabeth as an evidence that no word is impossible with God, then, but not until then, does she give her consent: *"Behold the handmaid of the Lord; be it done to me according to thy word."*

[56]Luke 1:26-38.

There was, then, a moment when the salvation of the world depended on the consent of Mary. Man could not be redeemed, satisfaction could not be made for sin, and grace obtained, without the Incarnation, and the Incarnation could not take place without the free, voluntary consent of this humble Jewish maiden. While, then, we are lost in admiration of the infinite condescension of God, that would do such honor to human nature as in some sort to place Himself in dependence on the will of one of our race to carry into effect His own purpose of infinite love and mercy, we cannot help feeling deep gratitude toward Mary for the consent she gave. We call her blessed for the great things He who is mighty has done to her,[57] and we bless her also for her own consent to the work of redemption. She gave to that work all she had: she gave her will; she gave her flesh; she gave her own Son to one long Passion of thirty-three years, to the agony in the garden, and to the death on the Cross.

It is true that God had selected her from all eternity to be His Mother and had filled her with grace, but neither the election nor the grace took away her free will or diminished the merit of her voluntary consent. She could

[57]Luke 1:49.

have refused. And does she deserve no love and gratitude from us, who have hope only through her flesh assumed by the Son of God, that she did not refuse? Can we say, in view of this fact, that she has no special relation to our redemption, no share in the work of our salvation? To say so would be simply to deny that we are redeemed and saved by God in the flesh; that the flesh, or human nature, of our Lord performs any office in the work of redemption and salvation. Wherefore, to refuse to honor Mary as connected with and sharing in that work is to deny that it is in His human nature that God redeems and saves us. This is either to deny redemption and salvation altogether, or to contend that God redeems and saves us in His divinity, that is, to contend that the divine nature suffered and died!

Mary is really the Mother of our Lord, for our Lord did in reality, not in appearance merely, come in the flesh. He is true God of God, and true man of the flesh of the Virgin. So, between Mary and Jesus there was and is the real relation of mother and son, and Mary still preserves all her maternal rights in regard to her Son, and He still owes her all filial love, reverence, and obedience. For if He is God, He is also man, and in His humanity has all that pertains to pure and sinless humanity. This would even justify in

Saint Worship and the Worship of Mary

some measure the expression — which, however, does not please us — said to have sometimes been used, not by the Church, but by some Catholics, in their ardent devotion to Mary: "Command thy Son." The Son of God in His humanity — not, of course, in His divine nature, nor in any matter that is proper to Him only in that nature — was subject to Mary here, and obeyed her. Therefore, her will, always one with God's will, because moved by the divine charity, is still regarded by Him as the will of His Mother and has that weight with Him that the right will of a mother must always have with a good, pious, and loving son.

We may then see the reasonableness of what many of our writers say, that Mary is the channel through which our Lord dispenses His graces, and that He dispenses none save through her intercession.[58] This, perhaps, is not precisely of faith, but it is a very general opinion of our Doctors. There is no reason it should not be so, and there are

[58]To this truth, the following illuminating consideration is added by Brownson's great contemporary, John Henry Newman, in writing of *The Difficulties of Anglicans* (cf. II, 105-106, 1888): that our Lady is able to intercede also for those who do not approach her; just as our Lord died even for those who did not know Him, His Mother prays even for those who do not know her. — ED.

many reasons we should hold it, aside from the authority of the Doctors and the general belief of the faithful. Mary is the channel through which all grace flows to us, inasmuch as she is the mother of the flesh in which God merited grace for us, redeems, sanctifies, and blesses us with everlasting life. But aside from this, to be made the channel through which God communicates His graces to us, whether the grace of conversion or of perseverance, is a high honor to her. And can we doubt that Jesus, as a loving Son, would delight to load with honors that dear Mother who had borne Him in her womb and in her arms, and nursed Him at her breast? Could He confer on her a higher honor than to make her intercession the condition on which He dispenses grace to us while in the flesh? Can we suppose His love for her would not induce Him to do so? Did He not, even before conceived in her womb, fill her with grace, make her all-beautiful? What, then, that can be communicated to a creature, will He withhold from her? He will withhold no good thing from those who love Him; certainly not, then, from His own dear Mother, who loves Him more than anyone else.

It would be in strict accordance with the plan of God's gracious providence, which includes the ministry of angels, and adopts throughout the principle of intercession as an integral part of it, for our Lord to place Mary first and to give her the blessed privilege of interceding in all cases, and of always having her intercession effectual. The whole, under this point of view, rests on the love that God bears toward His saints, and His delight in honoring them. It would seem, if we may so speak, that His love is so great that He exhausts His infinite wisdom in multiplying honors to them. And which of His saints should He so delight to honor as His own immaculate and loving Mother?

꩜

Chapter Twenty

Mary is our Mother and Queen

Mary is also *our* mother, the mother of all the faithful. They who never reflect on the mystery of the Incarnation, and who have no faith in redemption through the Cross, laugh at us when we call her our mother. Yet she *is* our mother and, to say the least, as truly our mother as was Eve herself.

Eutychianism is a heresy. The human nature hypostatically united to the divine remains forever distinct from it, and therefore our Lord remains forever God and man in one divine Person. By assuming our nature, the Son of God has made Himself our Brother. Now, of this human nature in Christ, Mary is the Mother; and she is as truly our mother, insofar as we, through this nature, become united to Him.

She is not our natural mother, but she is the mother of our nature in God, insofar as we were raised to brotherhood with Christ, her Son, and made through Him one with God. She is our spiritual mother. We cannot too often repeat that it is the Word made flesh, or God in the flesh, who redeems and saves or beatifies us. It is always through the incarnate Son that we have access to the Father, or that even the saints in Heaven behold Him in the Beatific Vision as He is. The life we as Christians live here is the life that proceeds from God in His humanity, and the life we hope to live hereafter proceeds from Him in the same sense. To suppose the saint here or hereafter separated from the flesh that God assumed in the womb of the Virgin would be to suppose his annihilation as a saint, as much as to suppose our separation from God as Creator would be to suppose the annihilation of our natural existence.

Here is the mystery of godliness that was manifest in the flesh. So, unless we can make it true that Mary is not the Mother of our Lord in His human nature, we cannot make it untrue that she is our spiritual mother. So long as spiritual life is dependent on God in His human nature, so long is Mary truly the mother of spiritual life. And so long as she is the mother of that life, so long is she our spiritual mother, and to be honored as such — and honored even more than our natural mother, for the spiritual life is infinitely more than the natural life. Mary is also our spiritual mother inasmuch as it has been through her intercession that we have been regenerated and hope to obtain the gift of perseverance.

Mary is called the Queen of Heaven — of Heaven and earth — universal queen. Our Lord is King, for to Him has all dominion been given. He is King, not merely as Son of God, in His divine nature, but He is King in His human nature, as Son of Mary. Her Son is King, so she, as mother of the King, is queen. As He loves and honors His Mother and must, as a good son, wish all creatures also to love and honor her, He must have crowned her queen and given her a formal title to the love, honor, and obedience due a queen.

Chapter Twenty-One

We honor Christ by honoring Mary

Here are considerations that, if taken in connection with the mystery of the Incarnation, will fully justify our warm devotion to Mary and the strongest expressions that, in the fervor of our piety, we can use. God has honored her and placed her above every other creature, next below Himself, has endowed her with all the graces a creature can receive, and has exalted her to a rank as near His own as she can hold without ceasing to be a creature. She is pure, spotless, all-beautiful, full of grace, full of sweet love, cooperating in her will in the whole work of redemption, and constantly interceding for sinners and for the perseverance of the regenerate.

What more can we say? What other creature can have higher, or anything like so high, claims upon our love and gratitude? And what can be more pleasing to her divine Son than for us to regard ourselves as her clients and to render her the highest honor in our power? Considering her relation as mother to our King, the love her Son bears her, the high honor He bestows on her, and the favors He delights constantly to show her, whose intercession can be more powerful, or whom can man invoke with more, or with equal, confidence?

The peculiar devotion of Catholics to Mary springs, as all must see, from our faith in the Incarnation. Granting that mystery, all is right and proper. And consequently, the fact that we insist on it bears witness to the world that we believe with a firm faith that that mystery is a reality, that Jesus has really come in the flesh, and that, by His flesh, or God in the flesh, we are saved. The worship of Mary is one perpetual festival in honor of that sacred mystery, and the prominent part assigned to Mary in all Catholic worship is only a proof of our faith that all in Christian redemption and salvation turns on the mystery of the Word made flesh. The daily practice of devotion to Mary as the Mother of God, aside from the special graces it obtains for us, keeps alive in our minds and in our hearts this mystery of mysteries, and our dependence on it for every good in the spiritual order. We cannot think of

Mary without thinking of Jesus. We cannot honor her without honoring Him as her Son, for here the honor of the Mother is from the Son, not the honor of the Son from the Mother.

We do not honor Mary as separated from her Son, but as His Mother, and for what she is, being His Mother. Her name brings at once to our mind His name, and the mystery of the Incarnation, the foundation of all our hope, the source of all our life. We do not connect her with the mystery of redemption as efficient cause, for the efficient cause is the infinite charity of the ever-adorable Trinity. But we do connect her with it as a medial cause, as an instrument, and as an instrument freely cooperating, and therefore as not without a moral share in the work and the glory of our salvation.

As long as we worship her, we can never forget the Lord who bought us, who has redeemed us with a price, with the price of His own blood. And indifference to her worship is always a sign of a want of love toward Him, and want of faith in the Incarnation as a reality. None of those who reject Mary's worship understand, or if they understand, believe, the doctrine of salvation through the Cross. Her worship is the best conceivable preservative of the essential Christian Faith, and to neglect it, as we see from history, is only to fall into unbelief and mere naturalism.

We do not honor Mary as God. We know that she is a creature and that it is only as a creature that we can honor her. The very foundation of the honor we give her is the fact that she is a creature. We honor her as the Mother of God, from whose womb He took His flesh, His created nature. The more we honor her, the more, therefore, are we reminded that she is not God, but is, like us, God's creature. We cannot call her our mother and assert that it is only through the flesh our Lord took from her womb that we come into brotherhood with Him, and are united to Him by a common nature, without distinctly asserting her to be a creature like ourselves. To suppose her divine, or any other than a true woman of our own race, would overthrow our whole faith in the mystery of the Incarnation and destroy all hopes of Heaven.

Chapter Twenty-Two

Worship of Mary preserves us from unbelief and impurity

Protestants call the worship we pay to our Lady *Mariolatry*. In the preceding section, this charge has been fully answered. The peculiar distinctive external worship of God is the offering of sacrifice. Those who have rejected the sacrifice of the Mass have retained nothing more than we offer to Mary and the saints. Consequently, they are unable to perceive any distinction between what they regard as the external worship of God, and that which we render to Him in His saints — that is, a worship of prayer and praise. But we have a sacrifice and are therefore able to distinguish between the highest honor we render to His saints and the supreme worship we render to Him, never to any creature.

Saint Worship and the Worship of Mary

The Protestant may speak of internal sacrifices, those of a broken heart and of inward justice, but these are only sacrifices by way of analogy, and what should always accompany the sacrifice proper. If the Protestant tells us that he worships God in the interior homage of contrition and submission of himself, we tell him, in return, that then he must not call the worship we render to Mary Mariolatry, because this homage and submission, in the sense he means, we never offer to her. If he has something in this interior homage that pertains to supreme worship, the worship of *latria*, he must bear in mind that we do not offer it to the saints, and therefore our worship of them is not idolatry. If he has not something of this sort, then he does not himself offer any worship proper to God, external or internal, and he therefore has in no sense any worship to offer to God of a higher order than that which we offer to Mary and the saints.

The worship of the saints, we conclude, is the worship of God in His works. The worship of Mary is the honoring of God in the mystery of the Incarnation. As God in both is infinitely adorable, the honor we render to the saints or to Mary can never be carried too high, and as it is always distinguishable in kind from that worship which we render to Him for what He is in Himself, as God our Creator,

Redeemer, and Supreme Good, it can never be idolatry, or detract from the honor due to Him alone. We love and honor God too little, but we cannot love and honor the saints too much. We are too weak, too cold, and too languid in our love for Jesus, but we cannot be too strong and fervid in our love for Mary, for we can never love and honor her so much as God Himself loves and honors her.

We need not say that works on the love and veneration of Mary can hardly be too much multiplied, for that love and veneration cannot be carried to excess. No doubt, wherever there is strong faith and lively devotion without proper instruction, there may chance to be manifested now and then something of superstition, whether the immediate object of worship be the saints or even God Himself, for there is nothing which men cannot abuse. But superstition, except as combined with idolatry and unbelief, or misbelief, is not one of the dangers of our times. And as the worship of Mary is the best preservative from idolatry, heresy, and unbelief, so is it the best preservative from superstition.

Those who love and honor Mary are not abettors of modern necromancy. Her devout children will not be found among those who call up the spirits of the dead and seek to be placed in communication with devils. The devils fly at her approach, and all lying spirits are silent in her presence. She is Queen of Heaven and Earth, and even rebellious spirits must tremble and bow before her. Demon-worship is undeniably reviving in the modern world, and there is no room to doubt that it is owing to the abandonment of the worship of Mary, which carries along with it the abandonment of the worship of her Son, the incarnate God. Where Mary is not loved and honored, Christ is not worshiped; and where Christ is not worshiped, the devils have the field all to themselves. The first symptom of apostasy from Christ and of a lapse into heathenism is the neglect of the worship of His most holy Mother and the rejection of that worship as superstition or idolatry, because that involves a rejection of the Incarnation, which comprises in itself all of Christianity.

In its bearings on Christian Faith and worship, then, we cherish the worship of Mary and are anxious to see devotion to her increase. But we are also anxious to see it increase as the best preservative against the moral dangers of our epoch. Mary is the mother of chaste love, and chaste love is that which, in our age, is most rare. The predominating sin of our times is impurity, at once the cause and the effect of the modern sentimental philosophy. The popular literature of the day is unchaste and impure.

Worship of Mary preserves us from unbelief

Catholic morality is scouted as impracticable and absurd; law is regarded as fallen into desuetude; intellect is derided; reason is looked upon as superfluous, if not tyrannical; and the heart is extolled as the representative of God on earth. Feeling is honored as the voice of the Most High, and whatever tends to restrain or control it is held to be a direct violation of the will of our Creator. Passion is deified, and nothing is held to be sacred but our transitory feelings. Hence, everywhere we find an impatience of restraint; a loud and indignant protest against all rule or measure in our affections and all those usages and customs of past times intended as safeguards of manners and morals; and a universal demand for liberty, which simply means unbounded license to follow our impure or perverted instincts and to indulge our most turbulent and unchaste passions, without shame or remorse.

The last, perhaps the only, remedy for this fearful state of things is to be sought in promoting and extending the worship of Mary. Society is lapsing, if it has not already lapsed, into the state in which Christianity found it some eighteen hundred years ago, and a new conversion of the Gentiles has become necessary. Christian society can be restored only by the same Faith and worship that originally created it. Jesus and Mary are now, as then, the only hope of the world, and their power and their goodwill remain undiminished. The worship of Mary as Mother of God redeemed the pagan world from its horrible corruptions, introduced and sustained the Christian family, and secured the fruits of the sacrament of marriage. It will do no less for our modern world, if cultivated; and we regard as one of the favorable signs that better times are at hand, the increasing devotion to Mary.

This is marked throughout the whole Catholic world, as is manifest from the intense interest that is felt in the probable approaching definition of the question of the Immaculate Conception.[59] Nowhere is the change in regard to devotion to Mary as the Mother of God more

[59]We must remind ourselves that Brownson wrote these words in 1853. On December 8 of the following year, Pope Pius IX issued the dogmatic letter *Ineffabilis Deus*, which, after tracing the doctrine through the Scriptures, and the teachings of the Church from the earliest ages, solemnly affirmed: "We declare, pronounce and define that the doctrine which holds that the Most Blessed Virgin Mary, at the first instant of her conception, was preserved immaculate from all stain of Original Sin, by the singular grace and privilege of the omnipotent God, in virtue of the merits of Jesus Christ, the Savior of mankind, has been revealed by God, and, therefore must be believed firmly and constantly by all the faithful." — ED.

striking than among the Catholics of Great Britain and of our own country. This devotion is peculiarly Catholic, and any increase of it is an indication of reviving life and fervor among Catholics. And if Catholics had only the life and fervor they should have, the whole world would soon bow in humble reverence at the foot of the Cross. It is owing to our deadness, our lack of zeal, our lack of true fervor in our devotions, that so many nations and such multitudes of souls are still held in the chains of darkness, under the dominion of Satan.

There are two ways in which the love and service of Mary will contribute to redeem society and restore Christian purity: the natural influence of such love and service on the heart of her worshipers, and the graces which in requital she obtains from her Son and bestows upon those who love her. Mary is the mother of chaste love. The nature of love is always to unite the heart to the object loved. Love always makes us like unto the beloved, and we always become like the object we really and sincerely worship. If we may say, "Like worshipers, like gods," we may with equal truth say, "Like gods, like worshipers." The love of Mary tends naturally, from the nature of all love, to unite us to her by a virtue kindred to her own. We cannot love her or dwell on her merits, her excellences, and her glories without being constantly led to imitate her virtues, to love and strive after her perfect purity, her deep humility, her profound submission, and her unreserved obedience. Her love checks all lawlessness of the affections, all turbulence of the passions, and all perturbation of the senses; fills the heart with sweet peace and a serene joy; restores to the soul its self-command; and maintains perfect order and tranquillity within. Something of this effect is produced whenever we love any truly virtuous person. If this is so when the beloved is but an ordinary mortal, how much more when the beloved, the one with whom we commune, and whose virtues we reverence and long to possess, is Mary, the Mother of God, the simplest and lowliest of handmaidens, but surpassing in true beauty, loveliness, and worth all the other creatures of God!

Undoubtedly the worship of Mary is restricted to Catholics and to those Catholics not undeserving of the name; but this is no objection to our general conclusion. We are too apt to forget that the Church is in the world, and that it is through her that society is redeemed. We are too apt to forget that the quiet and unobtrusive virtues of Catholics living in the midst of a hostile world are always powerful in their operations on that world, and that the world is converted, not by the direct efforts we make to convert it, but by the efforts we make to live as good Catholics and to save our own souls. The little handful of sincere and devout Catholics, the little family of sincere and earnest people devoted to Mary, seeking to imitate her virtues in their own little community, are as leaven hidden in three measures of meal.[60] Virtue goes forth from them and diffuses itself on all sides, until the whole is leavened. No matter how small the number, the fact that even some keep alive in the community the love and veneration of Mary, the true ideal of womanhood, the true patroness of the Christian family, the mother of chaste love, adorned with all the virtues, and to whom the Holy Spirit says, "Thou art all-fair, O my love,"[61] must have a redeeming effect on the whole community, and sooner or later must banish impurity and revive the love of holy purity and reverence for Catholic morality.

For, in the second place, the worship of Mary is profitable, not only by the subjective effect it has upon those who love her, but also by the blessings she obtains for them and, at their solicitation, for others. In these later times, we have almost lost sight of religion in its objective

[60]Cf. Matt. 13:33.

[61]Cant. 4:7 (RSV = Song of Sol. 4:7).

character. The world has ceased to believe in the Real Presence; it denies the whole sacramental character of Christianity and laughs at us when we speak of any sacrament as having any virtue not derived from the faith and virtue of the recipient. The whole non-Catholic world makes religion a purely subjective affair and deduces all its truth from the mind, and all its efficacy from the heart, that accepts and cherishes it, so that even in religion, which is a binding of man anew to God, man is everything, and God is nothing.

At bottom, that world is atheistical, at best Epicurean. It either denies God altogether or excludes Him from all care of the world He has created. It has no understanding of His providence, no belief in His abiding presence with His creatures, or His free and tender providence in their behalf. Faith, it assumes, is profitable only in its subjective operations, prayer only in its natural effect on the mind and heart of him who prays, and love only in its natural effect on the affections of the lover. This cold and atheistical philosophy is the enlightenment, the progress, of our age.

But we who are Christians know that it is false; we know that God is very near unto every one of us, is ever free to help us, and that there is nothing that He will not do for those who love Him truly and sincerely, and confide in Him, and in Him only.

Mary is the channel through which her divine Son dispenses all His graces and blessings to us, and He loves and delights to load with His favors all who love and honor her. Thus, to love and serve her is the way to secure His favor and to obtain those graces we need to resist the workings of concupiscence and to maintain the purity of our souls and of our bodies, which are the temple of God. She says, "I love them that love me";[62] we cannot doubt that she will favor with her always successful intercession those whom she loves. She will obtain grace for us to keep ourselves chaste and will, in requital of our love for her, obtain graces even for those without, so that they may be brought in and healed of their wounds and putrefying sores.

So, under either point of view, the love and worship of Mary, the Mother of God, a mother yet a virgin, always a virgin — Virgin most pure, most holy, most humble, most amiable, most loving, most merciful, most faithful, most powerful — cannot fail to enable us to overcome the terrible impurity of our age and to attain to the virtues now

[62]Prov. 8:17.

most needed for our own individual salvation and for the safety of society.

In this view of the case, we must feel that nothing is more important than the cultivation of the love and worship of Mary. She is our life, our sweetness, and our hope, and we must suffer no sneers of those without, no profane babblings about "Mariolatry" to move us or in the least to deter us from giving our hearts to Mary. We must fly to her protection as the child flies to his mother and seek our safety and our consolation in her love, in her maternal embrace.

Our help is in thee, sweet mother. Oh, protect us, thy children, and save us from the evil communications of this world, lost to virtue, and enslaved to the enemy of our souls!

❧

Orestes A. Brownson
(1803-1876)

"Man is an intelligence, or else he could not think," Orestes Brownson once wrote, "but he is a finite intelligence. His light is a true light, as far as it is light; but it is feeble and dim. It shines only a little way into the darkness, and even that way merely as a sudden flash, permitting us to see that there are objects there, but vanishing too soon to enable us to see what they are. It cannot enlighten all reality."[63]

Brownson spent many years searching for that hidden reality and then marveled at "the riches and beauty, the

[63]*Synthetic Philosophy, The Complete Works of Orestes A. Brownson*, Volume 1, 70.

life and grandeur, of God's universe" that transcend the material order.

Brownson was born in Stockbridge, Vermont. At the age of two, he lost his father and, because of financial difficulties, was sent to live among Congregationalists on a small farm in Royalton, Vermont, until he was fourteen. Although he had access to only a few books — all of them religious — he developed a love for reading, which led to his prolific literary career.

Brownson's spiritual search, which he traces in his book *The Convert: or, Leaves from My Experience*, was long and meandering. Raised by Congregationalists, he later joined the Presbyterian Church, became a Universalist preacher, then an independent minister, a Unitarian pastor, and pastor of a Congregational Church before he finally entered the Catholic Church with his family in 1844.

His writing and publishing career followed his religious journey. He edited the Universalist theological journal, *The Gospel Advocate*, published *The Boston Quarterly* as a Unitarian, and even wrote for the Transcendentalist magazine *The Dial*. His articles included philosophical and literary pieces, as well as political essays that made a name for him across the country.

Orestes A. Brownson

As a Catholic, he published *Brownson's Quarterly Review* and wrote articles for several publications, such as *Ave Maria* magazine, *The Catholic World* and *The American Catholic Quarterly Review*. His books include *The American Republic: Its Constitution, Tendencies, and Destiny* and *Conversations on Liberalism and the Church*.

Brownson died in 1876 in Detroit.

Thoroughly convinced, by his spiritual search, of the truths of the Church, Brownson became an eloquent Catholic apologist. The powerful arguments and lucid explanations in his writings continue to equip today's Catholics to understand and defend their Faith.

Sophia Institute Press®

Sophia Institute® is a nonprofit institution that seeks to restore man's knowledge of eternal truth, including man's knowledge of his own nature, his relation to other persons, and his relation to God. Sophia Institute Press® serves this end in numerous ways: it publishes translations of foreign works to make them accessible to English-speaking readers; it brings out-of-print books back into print; and it publishes important new books that fulfill the ideals of Sophia Institute®. These books afford readers a rich source of the enduring wisdom of mankind.

Sophia Institute Press® makes these high-quality books available to the general public by using advanced technology and by soliciting donations to subsidize its general publishing costs. Your generosity can help Sophia Institute

Press® to provide the public with editions of works containing the enduring wisdom of the ages. Please send your tax-deductible contribution to the address below. We also welcome your questions, comments, and suggestions.

For your free catalog, call:
Toll-free: 1-800-888-9344

or write:
Sophia Institute Press®
Box 5284, Manchester, NH 03108

or visit our website:
www.sophiainstitute.com

Sophia Institute® is a tax-exempt institution
as defined by the Internal Revenue Code,
Section 501(c)(3). Tax I.D. 22-2548708.